The Second Helvetic Confession

By

Heinrich Bullinger

First published in 1562

Published by Left of Brain Books

Copyright © 2023 Left of Brain Books

ISBN 978-1-397-66765-6

First Edition

All rights reserved. No part of this publication may be reproduced, distributed, or transmitted in any form or by any means, including photocopying, recording, or other electronic or mechanical methods, without the prior written permission of the publisher, except in the case of brief quotations permitted by copyright law. Left of Brain Books is a division of Left Of Brain Onboarding Pty Ltd.

PUBLISHER'S PREFACE

About the Book

"The Second Helvetic Confession Latin: Confessio Helvetica posterior gained a favourable hold on the Swiss churches, who had found the First Confession too short and too Lutheran. It was adopted by the Reformed Church not only throughout Switzerland but in Scotland (1566), Hungary (1567), France (1571), Poland (1578), and next to the Heidelberg Catechism is the most generally recognized Confession of the Reformed Church."

(Quote from wikipedia.org)

About the Author

Henrich Bullinger (1504 - 1575)

"Heinrich Bullinger (July 18, 1504 - September 17, 1575) was a Swiss reformer, the successor of Huldrych Zwingli as head of the Zurich church and pastor at Grossmünster. A much less controversial figure than John Calvin or Martin Luther, his importance has long been underestimated. Recent research showed, though, that he was one of the most influential Reformed theologians of the 16th century."

(Quote from wikipedia.org)

CONTENTS

PUBLISHER'S PREFACE
   OF THE HOLY SCRIPTURE BEING THE TRUE WORD OF GOD 1
   OF INTERPRETING THE HOLY SCRIPTURE; AND OF FATHERS, COUNCILS, AND TRADITIONS 4
   OF GOD, HIS UNITY AND TRINITY 7
   OF IDOLS OR IMAGES OF GOD, CHRIST AND THE SAINTS 9
   OF THE ADORATION, WORSHIP AND INVOCATION OF GOD THROUGH THE ONLY MEDIATOR JESUS CHRIST 11
   OF THE PROVIDENCE OF GOD 14
   OF THE CREATION OF ALL THINGS: OF ANGELS, THE DEVIL, AND MAN 17
   OF MAN'S FALL, SIN AND THE CAUSE OF SIN 19
   OF FREE WILL, AND THUS OF HUMAN POWERS 22
   OF THE PREDESTINATION OF GOD AND THE ELECTION OF THE SAINTS 26
   OF JESUS CHRIST, TRUE GOD AND MAN, THE ONLY SAVIOR OF THE WORLD 30
   OF THE LAW OF GOD 37
   OF THE GOSPEL OF JESUS CHRIST, OF THE PROMISES, AND OF THE SPIRIT AND LETTER 40
   OF REPENTANCE AND THE CONVERSION OF MAN 43
   OF THE TRUE JUSTIFICATION OF THE FAITHFUL 49
   OF FAITH AND GOOD WORKS, AND OF THEIR REWARD, AND OF MAN'S MERIT 53
   OF THE CATHOLIC AND HOLY CHURCH OF GOD, AND OF THE ONE ONLY HEAD OF THE CHURCH 58
   OF THE MINISTERS OF THE CHURCH, THEIR INSTITUTION AND DUTIES 68
   OF THE SACRAMENTS OF THE CHURCH OF CHRIST 80
   OF HOLY BAPTISM 87
   OF THE HOLY SUPPER OF THE LORD 90
   OF RELIGIOUS AND ECCLESIASTICAL MEETINGS 97

OF THE PRAYERS OF THE CHURCH, OF SINGING, AND OF CANONICAL HOURS 99
OF HOLY DAYS, FASTS AND THE CHOICE OF FOODS 101
OF CATECHIZING AND OF COMFORTING AND VISITING THE SICK 105
OF THE BURIAL OF THE FAITHFUL, AND OF THE CARE TO BE SHOWN FOR THE DEAD; OF PURGATORY, AND THE APPEARING OF SPIRITS 107
OF RITES, CEREMONIES AND THINGS INDIFFERENT 109
OF THE POSSESSIONS OF THE CHURCH 111
OF CELIBACY, MARRIAGE AND THE MANAGEMENT OF DOMESTIC AFFAIRS 112
OF THE MAGISTRACY 115

OF THE HOLY SCRIPTURE BEING THE TRUE WORD OF GOD

CANONICAL SCRIPTURE. We believe and confess the canonical Scriptures of the holy prophets and apostles of both Testaments to be the true Word of God, and to have sufficient authority of themselves, not of men. For God himself spoke to the fathers, prophets, apostles, and still speaks to us through the Holy Scriptures.

And in this Holy Scripture, the universal Church of Christ has the most complete exposition of all that pertains to a saving faith, and also to the framing of a life acceptable to God; and in this respect it is expressly commanded by God that nothing be either added to or taken from the same.

SCRIPTURE TEACHES FULLY ALL GODLINESS. We judge, therefore, that from these Scriptures are to be derived true wisdom and godliness, the reformation and government of churches; as also instruction in all duties of piety; and, to be short, the confirmation of doctrines, and the rejection of all errors, moreover, all exhortations according to that word of the apostle, "All scripture is inspired by God and profitable for teaching, for reproof," etc. (II Timothy 3:16-17). Again, "I am writing these instructions to you," says the apostle to Timothy, "So that you may know how one ought to behave in the household of God," etc. (I Timothy 3:14-15). SCRIPTURE IS THE WORD OF GOD. Again, the selfsame apostle to the Thessalonians: "When," says he, "You received the word of God which you heard from us, you accepted it, not as the word of men but as what it really is, the Word of God," etc. (I Thess. 2:13) For the

Lord himself has said in the gospel, "It is not you who speak, but the Spirit of my Father speaking through you"; therefore "He who hears you hears me, and he who rejects me rejects him who sent me" (Matt. 10:20; Luke 10:16; John 13:20)

THE PREACHING OF THE WORD OF GOD IS THE WORD OF GOD. Wherefore when this Word of God is now preached in the church by preachers lawfully called, we believe that the very Word of God is proclaimed, and received by the faithful; and that neither any other Word of God is to be invented nor is to be expected from heaven: and that now the Word itself which is preached is to be regarded, not the minister that preaches; for even if he be evil and a sinner, nevertheless the Word of God remains still true and good.

Neither do we think that therefore the outward preaching is to be thought as fruitless because the instruction in true religion depends on the inward illumination of the Spirit, or because it is written "And no longer shall each man teach his neighbor..., for they shall all know me" (Jer. 31:34), And "Neither he who plants nor he that waters is anything, but only God who gives the growth" (I Cor. 3:7). For although "No one can come to Christ unless he be drawn by the Father" (John 6:44), And unless the Holy Spirit inwardly illumines him, yet we know that it is surely the will of God that his Word should be preached outwardly also. God could indeed, by his Holy Spirit, or by the ministry of an angel, without the ministry of St. Peter, have taught Cornelius in the Acts; but, nevertheless, he refers him to Peter, of whom the angel speaking says, "He shall tell you what you ought to do."

INWARD ILLUMINATION DOES NOT ELIMINATE EXTERNAL PREACHING. For he that illuminates inwardly by giving men the Holy Spirit, the same one, by way of commandment, said unto his disciples, "Go into all the world, and preach the gospel to the whole creation" (Mark 16:15). And so in Phillippi, Paul preached the word outwardly to Lydia, a seller of purple goods; but the Lord inwardly opened the woman's heart (Acts 16:14). And the same Paul, after a beautiful development of his thought, in Romans 10:17 at length comes to the conclusion, "So faith comes from hearing and hearing from the Word of God by the preaching of Christ."

At the same time we recognize that God can illuminate whom and when he will, Even without the external ministry, for that is in his power; but we speak of the usual way of instructing men, delivered unto us from God, both by commandment and examples.

HERESIES. We therefore detest all the heresies of Artemon, the Manichaeans, the Valentinians, of Cerdon, and the Marcionites, who deny that the Scriptures proceeded from the Holy Spirit; or did not accept some parts of them, or interpolated and corrupted them.

APOCRYPHA. And yet we do not conceal the fact that certain books of the Old Testament were by the ancient authors called apocryphal, and by the others ecclesiastical; in as much as some would have them read in the churches, but not advanced as an authority from which the faith is to be established. As Augustine also, in his De Civitate Dei, book 18, ch. 38, remarks that "In the books of the Kings, the names and books of certain prophets are cited"; but he adds that "They are not in the canon"; and that "those books which we have suffice unto godliness."

OF INTERPRETING THE HOLY SCRIPTURE; AND OF FATHERS, COUNCILS, AND TRADITIONS

THE TRUE INTERPRETATION OF SCRIPTURE. The apostle peter has said that the Holy Scriptures are not of private interpretation (2 Pet. 1:20), and thus we do not allow all possible interpretations. Nor consequently do we acknowledge as the true or genuine interpretation of the Scriptures what is called the conception of the Roman Church, that is, what the defenders of the Roman Church plainly maintain should be thrust upon all for acceptance. But we hold that the interpretation of the Scripture to be orthodox and genuine which is gleaned from the Scriptures themselves (from the nature of the language in which they were written, likewise according to the circumstances in which they were set down, and expounded in the light of and unlike passages and of many and clearer passages) and which agree with the rule of faith and love, and contributes much to the glory of God and man's salvation.

INTERPRETATIONS OF THE HOLY FATHERS. Wherefore we do not despise the interpretations of the holy Greek and Latin fathers, nor reject their disputations and treatises concerning sacred matters as far as they agree with the Scriptures; but we modestly dissent from them when they are found to set down things differing from, or altogether contrary to, the Scriptures. Neither do we think that we do them any wrong in this matter; seeing that they all, with one consent, will not have their writings equated with the canonical Scriptures, but command us to prove how far they agree or disagree with them, and to accept what is in agreement and to reject what is in disagreement.

COUNCILS. And in the same order also we place the decrees and canons of councils.

Wherefore we do not permit ourselves, in controversies about religion or matters of faith, to urge our case with only the opinions of the fathers or decrees of councils; much less by received customs, or by the large number of those who share the same opinion, or by the prescription of a long time. Who Is The Judge? Therefore, we do not admit any other judge than God himself, who proclaims by the Holy Scriptures what is true, what is false, what is to be followed, or what to be avoided. So we do assent to the judgments of spiritual men which are drawn from the Word of God. Certainly Jeremiah and other prophets vehemently condemned the assemblies of priests which were set up against the law of God; and diligently admonished us that we should not listen to the fathers, or tread in their path who, walking in their own inventions, swerved from the law of God.

TRADITIONS OF MEN. Likewise we reject human traditions, even if they be adorned with high-sounding titles, as though they were divine and apostolical, delivered to the Church by the living voice of the apostles, and, as it were, through the hands of apostolical men to succeeding bishops which, when compared with the Scriptures, disagree with them; and by their disagreement show that they are not Apostolic at all. For as the apostles did not contradict themselves in doctrine, so the apostolic men did not set forth things contrary to the apostles. On the contrary, it would be wicked to assert that the apostles by a living voice delivered anything contrary to their writings. Paul affirms expressly that he taught the same things in all churches (I Cor. 4:17). And, again, "For we write you nothing but what you can read and understand." (II Cor. 1:13). Also, in another place, he testifies that he and his disciples - that is, apostolic men - walked in the same way, and jointly by the same Spirit did all things (II Cor. 12:18). Moreover, the Jews in former times had the traditions of their elders; but these traditions were severely rejected by the Lord, indicating that the keeping of them hinders God's law, and that God is worshipped in vain by such traditions (Matt. 15:1 ff.; Mark 7:1 ff).

OF GOD, HIS UNITY AND TRINITY

GOD IS ONE. We believe and teach that God is one in essence or nature, subsisting in himself, all sufficient in himself, invisible, incorporeal, immense, eternal, Creator of all things both visible and invisible, the greatest good, living, quickening and preserving all things, omnipotent and supremely wise, kind and merciful, just and true. Truly we detest many gods because it is expressly written: "The Lord your God is one Lord" (Deut.6:4). "I am the Lord your God. You shall have no other gods before me" (Ex. 20:2-3). "I am the Lord, and there is no other god besides me. Am I not the Lord, and there is no other God beside me? A righteous God and a Savior; there is none besides me" ((Isa. 45:5, 21). "The Lord, the Lord, a God merciful and gracious, slow to anger, and abounding in steadfast love and faithfulness" (Ex. 34:6).

GOD IS THREE. Notwithstanding we believe and teach that the same immense, one and indivisible God is in person inseparably and without confusion distinguished as Father, Son and Holy Spirit so, as the Father has begotten the Son from eternity, the Son is begotten by an ineffable generation, and the holy Spirit truly proceeds from them both, and the same from eternity and is to be worshipped with both.

Thus there are not three gods, but three persons, cosubstantial, coeternal, and coequal; distinct with respect to hypostases, and with respect to order, the one preceding the other yet without any inequality. For according to the nature or essence they are so joined together that they are one God, and the divine nature is common to the Father, Son and Holy Spirit.

For Scripture has delivered to us a manifest distinction of persons, the angel saying, among other things, to the Blessed Virgin, "The Holy Spirit will come upon you, and the power of the Most High will overshadow you; therefore the child to be born will be called holy, the Son of God" (Luke 1:35). And also in the baptism of Christ a voice is heard from heaven concerning Christ, saying, "This is my beloved Son" (Math. 3:17). The Holy Spirit also appeared in the form of a dove (John 1:32). And when the Lord himself commanded the apostles to baptize, he commanded them to baptize "in the name of the Father, and the Son, and the Holy Spirit" (Matt. 28:19). Elsewhere in the Gospel he said: "The Father will send the Holy Spirit in my name" (John 14:26), and again he said: "When the Counselor comes, whom I shall send to you from the Father, even the Spirit of truth, who proceeds from the Father, he will bear witness to me," etc. (John 15:26). In short, we receive the Apostles' Creed because it delivers to us the true faith.

HERESIES. Therefore we condemn the Jews and Mohammedans, and all those who blaspheme that sacred and adorable Trinity. We also condemn all heresies and heretics who teach that the Son and Holy Spirit are God in name only, and also that there is something created and subservient, or subordinate to another in the Trinity, and that their is something unequal in it, a greater or a less, something corporeal or corporeally conceived, something different with respect to character or will, something mixed or solitary, as if the Son and Holy Spirit were the affections and properties of one God the Father, as the Monarchians, Novatians, Praxeas, Patripassians, Sabellius, Paul of Samosata, Aetius, Macedonius, Anthropomorphites, Arius, and such like, have thought.

OF IDOLS OR IMAGES OF GOD, CHRIST AND THE SAINTS

IMAGES OF GOD. Since God as Spirit is in essence invisible and immense, he cannot really be expressed by any art or image. For this reason we have no fear pronouncing with Scripture that images of God are mere lies. Therefore we reject not only the idols of the Gentiles, but also the images of Christians.

IMAGES OF CHRIST. Although Christ assumed human nature, yet he did not on that account assume it in order to provide a model for carvers and painters. He denied that he had come "to abolish the law and the prophets" (Matt. 5:17). But images are forbidden by the law and the prophets" (Deut. 4:15; Isa. 44:9). He denied that his bodily presence would be profitable for the Church, and promised that he would be near us by his Spirit forever (John 16:7). Who, therefore, would believe that a shadow or likeness of his body would contribute any benefit to the pious? (II Cor. 5:5). Since he abides in us by his Spirit, we are therefore the temple of God (I Cor. 3:16). But "what agreement has the temple of God with idols?" (II Cor. 6:16).

IMAGES OF SAINTS. And since the blessed spirits and saints in heaven, while they lived here on earth, rejected all worship of themselves (Acts 3:12 f.; 14:11 ff.; Rev. 14:7; 22:9) and condemned images, shall anyone find it likely that the heavenly saints and angels are pleased with their own images before which men kneel. uncover their heads, and bestow other honors?

But in fact in order to instruct men in religion and to remind them of divine things and of their salvation, the Lord commanded the preaching of the Gospel (Mark 16:15) - not to paint and to teach the laity by means of pictures. Moreover, he instituted sacraments, but nowhere did he set up images.

THE SCRIPTURES OF THE LAITY. Furthermore, wherever we turn our eyes, we see the living and true creatures of God which, if they be observed, as is proper, make a much more vivid impression on the beholders than all images or vain, motionless, feeble and dead pictures made by men, of which the prophet truly said: "They have eyes, but do not see" (Ps. 115:5).

LACTANTIUS. Therefore we approved the judgment of Lactantius, and ancient writer, who says: "Undoubtedly no religion exists where there is an image."

EPIPHANIUS AND JEROME. We also assert that the blessed bishop Epiphanius did right when, finding on the doors of a church a veil on which was painted a picture supposedly of Christ or some saint, he ripped it down and took it away, because to see a picture of a man hanging in the Church of Christ was contrary to the authority of Scripture. Wherefore he charged that from henceforth no such veils, which were contrary to our religion, should be hung in the Church of Christ, and that rather such questionable things, unworthy of the Church of Christ and the faithful people, should be removed. Moreover, we approve of this opinion of St. Augustine concerning true religion: "Let not the worship of the works of men be a religion for us. For the artists themselves who make such things are better; yet we ought not to worship them" (De Vera Religione, cap. 55).

OF THE ADORATION, WORSHIP AND INVOCATION OF GOD THROUGH THE ONLY MEDIATOR JESUS CHRIST

GOD ALONE IS TO BE ADORED AND WORSHIPPED. We teach that the true God alone is to be adored and worshipped. This honor we impart to none other, according to the commandment of the Lord, "You shall worship the Lord your God and him only shall you serve" (Math. 4:10). Indeed, all the prophets severely inveighed against the people of Israel whenever they adored and worshipped strange gods, and not the only true God. But we teach that God is to be adored and worshipped as he himself has taught us to worship, namely, "in spirit and in truth" (John 4:23 f.), not with any superstition, but with sincerity, according to his Word; lest at anytime he should say to us: "Who has required these things from your hands?" (Isa. 1:12; Jer. 6:20). For Paul also says: "God is not served by human hands, as though he needed anything," etc. (Acts 17:25).

GOD ALONE IS TO BE INVOKED THROUGH THE MEDIATION OF CHRIST ALONE. In all crises and trials of our life we call upon him alone, and that by the mediation of our only mediator and intercessor, Jesus Christ. For we have been explicitly commanded: "Call upon me in the day of trouble; I will deliver you, and you shall glorify me" (Ps. 1:15). Moreover, we have a most generous promise from the Lord Who said: "If you ask anything of the Father, he will give it to you" (John 16:23), and: "Come to me, all who labor and are heavy laden and I will give you rest: (Matt 11:28). And since it is written: "How are men to call upon him in whom they have not believed?" (Rom. 10:14), and since we do believe in God alone, we assuredly call upon him alone, and we do so through Christ. For as the apostle says, "There is one God and there is one mediator between God and men, the man Christ Jesus? (I Tim. 2:5), and, "If any one does sin, we have an advocate with the Father, Jesus Christ the righteous," etc. (I John 2:1).

THE SAINTS ARE NOT TO BE ADORED, WORSHIPPED OR INVOKED. For this reason we do not adore, worship, or pray to the saints in heaven, or to other gods, and we do not acknowledge them as our intercessors or mediators before the Father in heaven. For God and Christ the Mediator are sufficient for us; neither do we give to others the honor that is due to God alone and to his Son, because he has expressly said: "My glory I give to no other: (Isa. 42:8), and because Peter has said: "There is no other name under heaven given among men by which we must be saved," except the name of Christ (Acts 4:12). In him, those who give their assent by faith do not seek anything outside Christ.

THE DUE HONOR TO BE RENDERED TO THE SAINTS. At the same time we do not despise the saints or think basely of them. For we acknowledge them to be living members of Christ and friends of God who have gloriously overcome the flesh and the world. Hence we love them as brothers, and also honor them; yet not with any kind of worship but by an honorable opinion of them and just praises of them. We also imitate them. For with ardent longings and supplications we earnestly desire to be imitators of their faith and virtues, to share eternal salvation with them, to dwell eternally with them in the presence of God, and to rejoice with them in Christ. And in this respect we approve of the opinion of St. Augustine in De Vera Religione: "Let not our religion be the cult of men who have died. For if they have lived holy lives, they are not to be thought of as seeking such honors; on the contrary, they want us to worship him by whose illumination they rejoice that we are fellow-servants of his merits. They are therefore to be honored by the way of imitation, but not to be adored in a religious manner," etc.

RELICS OF THE SAINTS. Much less do we believe that the relics of the saints are to be adored and reverenced. Those ancient saints seemed to have sufficiently honored their dead when they decently committed their remains to the earth after the spirit had ascended on high. And they thought that the most noble relics of their ancestors were their virtues, their doctrine, and their faith. Moreover, as they commend these "relics" when praising the dead, so they strive to copy them during their life on earth.

SWEARING BY GOD'S NAME ALONE. These ancient men did not swear except by the name of the only God, Yahweh, as prescribed by the divine law. Therefore, as it is forbidden to swear by the names of strange gods (Ex. 23:;13; Deut. 10:20), so we do not perform oaths to the saints that are demanded of us. We therefore reject in all these matters a doctrine that ascribes much too much to the saints in heaven.

OF THE PROVIDENCE OF GOD

ALL THINGS ARE GOVERNED BY THE PROVIDENCE OF GOD. We believe that all things in heaven and on earth, and in all creatures, are preserved and governed by the providence of this wise, eternal and almighty God. For David testifies and says: "The Lord is high above all nations, and his glory above the heavens! Who is like the Lord our God, who is seated on high, who looks far down upon the heavens and the earth?" (Ps. 113:4 ff.). Again: "Thou searchest out...all my ways. Even before a word is on my tongue, lo, O Lord, Thou knowest it altogether" (Ps. 139:3 f.). Paul also testifies and declares: "In him we live and move and have our being" (Acts 17:28), and "from him and through him and to him are all things" (Rom. 11:36). Therefore Augustine most truly and according to Scripture declared in his book De Agone Christi, cap. 8, "The Lord said, 'Are not two sparrows sold for a penny? And not one of them will fall to the ground without your Father's will'" (Matt. 10:29). By speaking thus he wanted to show that what men regard as of least value is governed by God's omnipotence. For he who is the truth says that the birds of the air are fed by him and lilies of the field are clothed by him; he also says that the hairs of our head are numbered (Matt. 6:26 ff.).

THE EPICUREANS. We therefore condemn the Epicureans who deny the providence of God, and all those who blasphemously say that God is busy with the heavens and neither sees nor cares about us and our affairs. David, the royal prophet, also condemned this when he said: "O Lord, how long shall the wicked exult? They say, "The Lord does not see; the God of Jacob does not perceive." Understand, O dullest of the people!

Fools, when will you be wise? He who planted the ear, does he not hear? He who formed the eye, does he not see?" (Ps. 94:3, 7-9).

MEANS NOT TO BE DESPISED. Nevertheless, we do not spurn as useless the means by which divine providence works, but we teach that we are to adapt ourselves to them in so far as they are recommended to us in the Word of God. Wherefore we disapprove of the rash statements of those who say that if all things are managed by the providence of God, then our efforts and endeavors are in vain. It will be sufficient if we leave everything to the governance of divine providence, and we will not have to worry about anything or do anything. For although Paul understood that he sailed under the providence of God who had said to him: "You must bear witness also at Rome" (Acts 23:11), and in addition had given him the promise, "There will be no loss of life among you...and not a hair is to perish from the head of any of you" (Acts 27:22,34), yet when the sailors were nevertheless thinking about abandoning ship the same Paul said to the centurion and the soldiers: "Unless these men stay in the ship, you cannot be saved" (Acts 27:31). For God, who has appointed to everything its end, has ordained the beginning and the means by which it reaches its goal. The heathen ascribe things to blind fortune and uncertain chance. But St. James does not want us to say: "Today or tomorrow we will go into such and such a town and trade," but adds: "Instead you ought to say, `If the Lord wills, we shall live and we shall do this or that' " (James 4:13, 15). And Augustine says: "Everything which to vain men seems to happen in nature by accident, occurs only by his Word, because it happens only at his command" (Enarrationes in Psalmos 148). Thus it seemed to happen by mere chance when Saul, while seeking his father's asses, unexpectedly fell in with the prophet Samuel. But previously the Lord had said to the prophet: "Tomorrow I will send to you a man from the land of Benjamin" (I Sam 9:15).

OF THE CREATION OF ALL THINGS: OF ANGELS, THE DEVIL, AND MAN

GOD CREATED ALL THINGS. This good and almighty God created all things, both visible and invisible, by his co-eternal Word, and preserves them by his co-eternal Spirit, as David testified when he said: "By the word of the Lord the heavens were made, and all their host by the breath of his mouth" (Ps. 33:6). And, as Scripture says, everything that God had made was very good, and was made for the profit and use of man. Now we assert that all those things proceed from one beginning. MANICHAEANS AND MARCIONITES. Therefore, we condemn the Manichaeans and Marcionites who impiously imagined two substances and natures, one good and the other evil; also two beginnings and two gods contrary to each other, a good and an evil one.

OF ANGELS AND THE DEVIL. Among all creatures, angels and men are most excellent. Concerning angels, Holy Scripture declares: "who makest the winds thy messengers, fire and flame thy ministers" (Ps 104:4). Also it says: "Are they not all ministering spirits sent forth to serve, for the sake of those who are to obtain salvation?" (Heb. 1:14). Concerning the Devil, the Lord Jesus Himself testifies: "He was a murderer from the beginning, and has nothing to do with the truth, because there is no truth in him. When he lies, he speaks according to his own nature, for he is a liar and the father of lies" (John 8:44). Consequently we teach that some angels persisted in obedience and were appointed for faithful service to God and men, but others fell of their own free will and were cast into destruction, becoming enemies of all good and of the faithful, etc....

OF MAN. Now concerning, Scripture says that in the beginning he was made good according to the image and likeness of God; that God placed him in paradise and made all thing subject to him (Gen. chp 2). This is what David magnificently sets forth in Psalm 8. Moreover, God gave him a wife and blessed them. We also affirm that man consists of two different substances in one person: an immortal soul which, when separate from the body, neither sleeps nor dies, and a mortal body which will nevertheless be raised up from the dead at the last judgement, in order that then the whole man, either in life or in death, abide forever.

THE SECTS. We condemn all who ridicule or by subtle arguments cast doubt upon the immortality of the soul, or who say that the soul sleeps or is a part of God. In short, we condemn all opinions of all men, however many, that depart from what has been delivered unto us by the Holy Scriptures in the Apostolic Church of Christ concerning creation, angels, and demons, and man.

OF MAN'S FALL, SIN AND THE CAUSE OF SIN

THE FALL OF MAN. In the beginning, man was made according to the image of God, in righteousness and true holiness, good and upright. But when at the instigation of the serpent and by his own fault he abandoned goodness and righteousness, he became subject to sin, death and various calamities. And what he became by the fall, that is, subject to sin, death and various calamities, so are all those who have descended from him.

SIN. By sin we understand that innate corruption of man which has been derived or propagated in us all from our first parents, by which we, immersed in perverse desires and averse to all good, are inclined to all evil. Full of all wickedness, distrust, contempt and hatred of God, we are unable to do or even to think anything good of ourselves. Moreover, even as we grow older, so by wicked thoughts, words and deeds committed against God's law, we bring forth corrupt fruit worthy of an evil tree (Matt. 12:33 ff.). For this reason by our own deserts, being subject to the wrath of God, we are liable to just punishment, so that all of us would have been cast away by God if Christ, the Deliverer, had not brought us back.

DEATH. By death we understand not only bodily death, which all of us must once suffer on account of sins, but also eternal punishment due to our sins and corruption. For the apostle says: "We were dead through trespasses and sins...and were by nature children of wrath, like the rest of mankind. But God, who is rich in mercy...even when we were dead through our trespasses, made us alive together with Christ" (Eph. 2:1 ff.)

Also: "As sin came into the world through one man and death through sin, and so death spread to all men because all men sinned" (Rom. 5:12).

ORIGINAL SIN. We therefore acknowledge that there is original sin in all men.

ACTUAL SINS. We acknowledge that all other sins which arise from it are called and truly are sins, no matter by what name they may be called, whether mortal, venial or that which is said to be the sin against the Holy Spirit which is never forgiven (Mark 3:29; I John 5:16). We also confess that sins are not equal; although they arise from the same fountain of corruption and unbelief, some are more serious than others. As the Lord said, it will be more tolerable for Sodom than for the city that rejects the word of the Gospel (Matt. 10:14 f.; 11:20 ff.).

THE SECTS. We therefore condemn all who have taught contrary to this, especially Pelagius and all Pelagians, together with the Jovinians who, with the Stoics, regard all sins as equal. In this whole matter we agree with St. Augustine who derived and defended his view from Holy Scriptures. Moreover, we condemn Florinus and Blastus, against whom Irenaeus wrote, and all who make God the author of sin.

GOD IS NOT THE AUTHOR OF SIN, AND HOW FAR HE IS SAID TO HARDEN. It is expressly written: "Thou art not a God who delights in wickedness. Thou hatest all evildoers. Thou destroyest those who speak lies" (Ps. 5:4 ff.). And again: "When the devil lies, he speaks according to his own nature, for he is a liar and the father of lies" (John 8:44). Moreover, there is enough sinfulness and corruption in us that it is not necessary for God to infuse into us a new or still greater perversity. When, therefore, it is said in Scripture that God hardens, blinds and delivers up to a reprobate mind, it is to be understood that God does it by a just judgment as a just Judge and Avenger. Finally, as often as God in Scripture is said or seems to do something evil, it is not thereby said that man does not do evil, but that God permits it and does not prevent it, according to his just judgment, who could prevent it if he wished, or because he turns man's evil into good, as he did in the case of the sin of Joseph's brethren, or because he governs sins lest they break out and rage more than is appropriate. St. Augustine writes in his Enchiridion: "What happens contrary to his will occurs, in a wonderful and ineffable way, not apart from his will. For it would not happen if he did not allow it. And yet he does not allow it unwillingly but willingly. But he who is good would not permit evil to be done, unless, being omnipotent, he could bring good out of evil." Thus wrote Augustine.

CURIOUS QUESTIONS. Other questions, such as whether God willed Adam to fall, or incited him to fall, or why he did not prevent the fall, and similar questions, we reckon among curious questions (unless perchance the wickedness of heretics or of other churlish men compels us also to explain them out of the Word of God, as the godly teachers of the Church have frequently done), knowing that the Lord forbade man to eat of the forbidden fruit and punished his transgression. We also know that what things are done are not evil with respect to the providence, will, and the power of God, but in respect of Satan and our will opposing the will of God.

OF FREE WILL, AND THUS OF HUMAN POWERS

IN this matter, which has always produced many conflicts in the Church, we teach that a threefold condition or state of man is to be considered.

WHAT MAN WAS BEFORE THE FALL. There is the state in which man was in the beginning before the fall, namely, upright and free, so that he could both continue in goodness and decline to evil. However, he declined to evil, and has involved himself and the whole human race in sin and death, as has been said already.

WHAT MAN WAS AFTER THE FALL. Then we are to consider what man was after the fall. To be sure, his reason was not taken from him, nor was he deprived of will, and he was not entirely changed into a stone or a tree. But they were so altered and weakened that they no longer can do what they could before the fall. For the understanding is darkened, and the will which was free has become an enslaved will. Now it serves sin, not unwillingly but willingly. And indeed, it is called a will, not an unwill (ing). [Etenim voluntas, non noluntas dicitur.]

MAN DOES EVIL BY HIS OWN FREE WILL. Therefore, in regard to evil or sin, man is not forced by God or by the devil but does evil by his own free will, and in this respect he has a most free will. But when we frequently see that the worst crimes and designs of men are prevented by God from reaching their purpose, this does not take away man's freedom in doing evil, but God by his own power prevents what man freely planned otherwise. Thus

Joseph's brothers freely determined to get rid of him, but they were unable to do it because something else seemed good to the counsel of God.

MAN IS NOT CAPABLE OF GOOD Per Se. In regard to goodness and virtue man's reason does not judge rightly of itself concerning divine things. For the evangelical and apostolic Scripture requires regeneration of whoever among us wishes to be saved. Hence our first birth from Adam contributes nothing to out salvation. Paul says: "The unspiritual man does not receive the gifts of the Spirit of God," etc. (I Cor. 2:14). And in another place he denies that we of ourselves are capable of thinking anything good (II Cor. 3:5) Now it is known that the mind or intellect is the guide of the will, and when the guide is blind, it is obvious how far the will reaches. Wherefore, man not yet regenerate has no free will for good, no strength to perform what is good. The Lord says in the Gospel: "Truly, truly, I say to you, everyone who commits sin is a slave to sin" (John 8:34). And the apostle Paul says: "The mind that is set on the flesh is hostile to God; it does not submit to God's law, indeed it cannot" (Rom. 8:7). Yet in regard to earthly things, fallen man is not entirely lacking in understanding.

UNDERSTANDING OF THE ARTS. For God in his mercy has permitted the powers of the intellect to remain, though differing greatly from what was in man before the fall. God commands us to cultivate our natural talents, and meanwhile adds both gifts and success. And it is obvious that we make no progress in all the arts without God's blessing. In any case, Scripture refers all the arts to God; and, indeed, the heathen trace the origin of the arts to the gods who invented them.

OF WHAT KIND ARE THE POWERS OF THE REGENERATE, AND IN WHAT WAY THEIR WILLS ARE FREE. Finally, we must see whether the regenerate have free wills, and to what extent. In regeneration the understanding is illumined by the Holy Spirit in order that it many understand both the mysteries and the will of God. And the will itself is not only changed by the Spirit, but it is also equipped with faculties so that it wills and is able to do the good of its own accord (Rom. 8:1ff.). Unless we grant this, we will deny Christian liberty and introduce a legal bondage. But the prophet has God saying: "I will put my law within them, and I will write it upon their hearts" (Jer. 31:33; Ezek. 36:26f.). The Lord also says in the Gospel: "If the Son makes you free, you will be free indeed" (John 8:36). Paul also writes to the Philippians: "It has been granted to you that for the sake of Christ you should not only believe in him but also suffer for his sake" (Phil. 1:29). Again: "I am sure that he who began a good work in you will bring it to completion at the day of Jesus Christ" (v. 6). Also: "God is at work in you, both to will and to work for his good pleasure" (ch. 2:13).

THE REGENERATE WORK NOT ONLY PASSIVELY BUT ACTIVELY. However, in this connection we teach that there are two things to be observed: First, that the regenerate, in choosing and doing good, work not only passively but actively. For they are moved by God that they may do themselves what they do. For Augustine rightly adduces the saying that "God is said to be our helper. But no one can be helped unless he does something." The Manichaeans robbed man of all activity and made him like a stone or a block of wood.

THE FREE WILL IS WEAK IN THE REGENERATE. Secondly, in the regenerate a weakness remains. For since sin dwells in us, and in the regenerate the flesh struggles against the Spirit till the end of our lives, they do not easily accomplish in all things what they had planned. These things are confirmed by the apostle in Rom., ch. 7, and Gal., ch. 5. Therefore that free will is weak in us on account of the remnants of the old Adam and of innate human corruption remaining in us until the end of our lives. Meanwhile, since the powers of the flesh and the remnants of the old man are not so efficacious that they wholly extinguish the work of the Spirit, for that reason the faithful are said to be free, yet so that they acknowledge their infirmity and do not glory at all in their free will. For believers ought always to keep in mind what St. Augustine so many times inculcated according to the apostle: "What have you that you did not receive? If then you received it, why do you boast as if it were not a gift?" To this he adds that what we have planned does not immediately come to pass. For the issue of things lies in the hand of God. This is the reason Paul prayed to the Lord to prosper his journey (Rom. 1:10). And this also is the reason the free will is weak.

IN EXTERNAL THINGS THERE IS LIBERTY. Moreover, no one denies that in external things both the regenerate and the unregenerate enjoy free will. For man has in common with other living creatures (to which he is not inferior) this nature to will some things and not to will others. Thus he is able to speak or to keep silent, to go out of his house or to remain at home, etc. However, even here God's power is always to be observed, for it was the cause that Balaam could not go as far as he wanted (Num., ch. 24), and Zacharias upon returning from the temple could not speak as he wanted (Luke, ch.1).

HERESIES. In this matter we condemn the Manichaeans who deny that the beginning of evil was for man [created] good, from his free will. We also condemn the Pelagians who assert that an evil man has sufficient free will to do the good that is commanded. Both are refuted by Holy Scripture which says to the former, "God made man upright" and to the latter, "If the Son makes you free, you will be free indeed" (John 8:36).

OF THE PREDESTINATION OF GOD AND THE ELECTION OF THE SAINTS

GOD HAS ELECTED US OUT OF GRACE. From eternity God has freely, and of his mere grace, without any respect to men, predestinated or elected the saints whom he wills to save in Christ, according to the saying of the apostle, "God chose us in him before the foundation of the world" (Eph. 1:4). And again: "Who saved us and called an with a holy calling, not in virtue of our works but in virtue of his own purpose and the grace which he gave us in Christ Jesus ages ago, and now has manifested through the appearing of our Savior Christ Jesus" (II Tim. 1:9 f.).

WE ARE ELECTED OR PREDESTINATED IN CHRIST. Therefore, although not on account of any merit of ours, God has elected us, not directly, but in Christ, and on account of Christ, in order that those who are now engrafted into Christ by faith might also be elected. But those who were outside Christ were rejected, according to the word of the apostle, "Examine yourselves, to see whether you are holding to your faith. Test yourselves. Do you not realize that Jesus Christ is in you? -- unless indeed you fail to meet the test!" (II Cor. 13:5).

WE ARE ELECTED FOR A DEFINITE PURPOSE. Finally, the saints are chosen in Christ by God for a definite purpose, which the apostle himself explains when he says, "He chose us in him for adoption that we should be holy and blameless before him in love. He destined us for adoption to be his sons through Jesus Christ that they should be to the praise of the glory of his grace" (Eph. 1:4 ff.).

WE ARE TO HAVE A GOOD HOPE FOR ALL. And although God knows who are his, and here and there mention is made of the small number of elect, yet we must hope well of all, and not rashly judge any man to be a reprobate. For Paul says to the Philippians, "I thank my God for you all" (now he speaks of the whole Church in Phillippi), "because of your fellowship in the Gospel, being persuaded that he who began a good work in you will bring it to completion at the day of Jesus Christ. It is also right that I have this opinion of you all" (Phil. 1:3 ff.).

WHETHER FEW ARE ELECT. And when the Lord was asked whether there were few that should be saved, he does not answer and tell them that few or many should be saved or damned, but rather he exhorts every man to "strive to enter by the narrow door" (Luke 13:24): as if he should say, It is not for you curiously to inquire about these matters, but rather to endeavor that you may enter into heaven by the straight way.

WHAT IN THIS MATTER IS TO BE CONDEMNED. Therefore we do not approve of the impious speeches of some who say, "Few are chosen, and since I do not know whether I am among the number of the few, I will enjoy myself." Others say, "If I am predestinated and elected by God, nothing can hinder me from salvation, which is already certainly appointed for me, no matter what I do. But if I am in the number of the reprobate, no faith or repentance will help me, since the decree of God cannot be changed. Therefore all doctrines and admonitions are useless." Now the saying of the apostle contradicts these men: "The Lord's servant must be ready to teach, instructing those who oppose him, so that if God should grant that they repent to know the truth, they may recover from the snare of the devil, after being held captive by him to do his will" (II Tim. 2:23 ff.).

ADMONITIONS ARE NOT IN VAIN BECAUSE SALVATION PROCEEDS FROM ELECTION. Augustine also shows that both the grace of free election and the predestination, and also salutary admonitions and doctrines, are to be preached (Lib. de Dono Perseverantiae, cap. 14 ff.).

WHETHER WE ARE ELECTED. We therefore find fault with those who outside of Christ ask whether they are elected. [Ed. 1568 reads: "whether they are elected from eternity?"] And what has God decreed concerning them before all eternity? For the preaching of the Gospel is to be heard, and it is to be believed; and it is to be held as beyond doubt that if you believe and are in Christ, you are elected. For the Father has revealed unto us in Christ the eternal purpose of his predestination, as I have just now shown from the apostle in II Tim. 1:9-10. This is therefore above all to be taught and considered, what great love of the Father toward us is revealed to us in Christ. We must hear what the Lord himself daily preaches to us in the Gospel, how he calls and says: "Come to me all who labor and are heavy-laden, and I will give you rest" (Matt. 11:28). "God so loved the world, that he gave his only Son, that whoever believes in him should not perish, but have eternal life" (John 3:16). Also, "It is not the will of my Father that one of these little ones should perish" (Matt. 18:14).

Let Christ, therefore be the looking glass, in whom we may contemplate our predestination. We shall have a sufficiently clear and sure testimony that we are inscribed in the Book of Life if we have fellowship with Christ, and he is ours and we are his in true faith.

TEMPTATION IN REGARD TO PREDESTINATION. In the temptation in regard to predestination, than which there is scarcely any other more dangerous, we are confronted by the fact that God's promises apply to all the faithful, for he says: "Ask, and everyone who seeks, shall receive" (Luke 11:9 f.) This finally we pray, with the whole Church of God, "Our Father who art in heaven" (Matt. 6:9), both because by baptism we are ingrafted into the body of Christ, and we are often fed in his Church with his flesh and blood unto life eternal. Thereby, being strengthened, we are commanded to work out our salvation with fear trembling, according to the precept of Paul.

OF JESUS CHRIST, TRUE GOD AND MAN, THE ONLY SAVIOR OF THE WORLD

CHRIST IS TRUE GOD. We further believe and teach that the Son of God, our Lord Jesus Christ, was predestinated or foreordained from eternity by the Father to be the Savior of the world. And we believe that he was born, not only when he assumed flesh of the Virgin Mary, and not only before the foundation of the world was laid, but by the Father before all eternity in an inexpressible manner. For Isaiah said: "Who can tell his generation?" (Ch. 53:8). And Micah says: "His origin is from of old, from ancient days" (Micah 5:2). And John said in the Gospel: "In the beginning was the Word, and the Word was with God, and the Word was God," etc. (Ch. 1:1). Therefore, with respect to his divinity the Son is coequal and consubstan-tial with the Father; true God (Phil. 2:11), not only in name or by adoption or by any merit, but in substance and nature, as the apostle John has often said: "This is the true God and eternal life" (I John 5:20). Paul also says: "He appointed the Son the heir of all things, through whom also he created the world. He reflects the glory of God and bears the very stamp of his nature, upholding all things by his word of power" (Heb. 1:2 f.). For in the Gospel the Lord himself said: "Father, glorify Thou me in Thy own presence with the glory which I had with Thee before the world was made" (John 17:5). And in another place in the Gospel it is written: "The Jews sought all the more to kill him because he...called God his Father, making himself equal with God" (John 5:18).

THE SECTS. We therefore abhor the impious doctrine of Arius and the Arians against the Son of God, and especially the blasphemies of the Spaniard, Michael Servetus, and all his followers, which Satan through them has, as it were, dragged up out of hell and has most audaciously and impiously spread abroad in the world.

CHRIST IS TRUE MAN, HAVING REAL FLESH. We also believe and teach that the eternal Son of the eternal God was made the Son of man, from the seed of Abraham and David, not from the coitus of a man, as the Ebionites said, but was most chastely conceived by the Holy Spirit and born of the ever virgin Mary, as the evangelical history carefully explains to us (Matt., ch. 1). And Paul says: "he took not on him the nature of angels, but of the seed of Abraham." Also the apostle John says that woever does not believe that Jesus Christ has come in the flesh, is not of God. Therefore, the flesh of Christ was neither imaginary not brought from heaven, as Valentinus and Marcion wrongly imagined.

A RATIONAL SOUL IN CHRIST. Moreover, our Lord Jesus Christ did not have a soul bereft of sense and reason, as Apollinaris thought, nor flesh without a soul, as Eunomius taught, but a soul with its reason, and flesh with its senses, by which in the time of his passion he sustained real bodily pain, as himself testified when he said: "My soul is very sorrowful, even to death" (Matt. 26:38). And, "Now is my soul troubled" (John 12:27).

TWO NATURES IN CHRIST. We therefore acknowledge two natures or substances, the divine and the human, in one and the same Jesus Christ our Lord (Heb., ch. 2). And we say that these are bound and united with one another in such a way that they are not absorbed, or confused, or mixed, but are united or joined together in one person the properties of the natures being unimpaired and permanent.

NOT TWO BUT ONE CHRIST. Thus we worship not two but one Christ the Lord. We repeat: one true God and man. With respect to his divine nature he is consubstantial with the Father, and with respect to the human nature he is consubstantial with us men, and like us in all things, sin excepted (Heb. 4:15).

THE SECTS. And indeed we detest the dogma of the Nestorians who make two of one Christ and dissolve the unity of the Person. Likewise we thoroughly execrate the madness of Eutyches and of the Monothelites or Monophysites who destroy the property of the human nature.

THE DIVINE NATURE OF CHRIST IS NOT PASSIBLE, AND THE HUMAN NATURE IS NOT EVERYWHERE. Therefore, we do not in any way teach that the divine nature in Christ has suffered or that Christ according to his human nature is still in this world and thus is everywhere. For neither do we think or teach that the body of Christ ceased to be a true body after his glorification, or was deified, and deified in such a way that it laid aside its properties as regards body and soul, and changed entirely into a divine nature and began to be merely one substance.

THE SECTS. Hence we by no means approve of or accept the strained, confused and obscure subtleties of Schwenkfeldt and of similar sophists with their self-contradictory arguments; neither are we Schwenkfeldians.

OUR LORD TRULY SUFFERED. We believe, moreover, that our Lord Jesus Christ truly suffered and died for us in the flesh, as Peter says (I Peter 4:1). We abhor the most impious madness of the Jacobites and all the Turks who execrate the suffering of the Lord. At the same time we do not deny that the Lord of glory was crucified for us, according to Paul's words (I Cor. 2:8).

IMPARTATION OF PROPERTIES. We piously and reverently accept and use the impartation of properties which is derived from Scripture and which has been used by all antiquity in explaining and reconciling apparently contradictory passages.

CHRIST IS TRULY RISEN FROM THE DEAD. We believe and teach that the same Jesus Christ our Lord, in his true flesh in which he was crucified and died, rose again from the dead, and that not another flesh was raised other than the one buried, or that a spirit was taken up instead of the flesh, but that he retained his true body. Therefore, while his disciples thought they saw the spirit of the Lord, he showed them his hands and feet which were marked by the prints of the nails and wounds, and added: "See my hands and my feet, that it is I myself; handle me, and see, for a spirit has not flesh and bones as you see that I have" (Luke 24:39).

CHRIST IS TRULY ASCENDED INTO HEAVEN. We believe that our Lord Jesus Christ, in his same flesh, ascended above all visible heavens into the highest heaven, that is, the dwelling-place of God and the blessed ones, at the right hand of God the Father. Although it signifies an equal participation in glory and majesty, it is also taken to be a certain place about which the Lord, speaking in the Gospel, says: "I go to prepare a place for you" (John 14:2). The apostle Peter also says: "Heaven must receive Christ until the time of restoring all things" (Acts 3:21). And from heaven the same Christ will return in judgment, when wickedness will then be at its greatest in the world and when the Antichrist, having corrupted true religion, will fill up all things with superstition and impiety and will cruelly lay waste the Church with bloodshed and flames (Dan., ch. 11). But Christ will come again to claim his own, and by his coming to destroy the Antichrist, and to judge the living and the dead (Acts 17:31). For the dead will rise again (I Thess. 4:14 ff.), and those who on that day (which is unknown to all creatures [Mark 13:32]) will be alive will be changed "in the twinkling of an eye," and all the faithful will be caught up to meet Christ in the air, so that then they may enter with him into the blessed dwelling-places to live forever (I Cor. 15:51 f.). But the unbelievers and ungodly will descend with the devils into hell to burn forever and never to be redeemed from torments (Matt. 25:46).

THE SECTS. We therefore condemn all who deny a real resurrection of the flesh (II Tim. 2:18), or who with John of Jerusalem, against whom Jerome wrote, do not have a correct view of the glorification of bodies. We also condemn those who thought that the devil and all the ungodly would at some time be saved, and that there would be an end to punishments. For the Lord has plainly declared: "Their fire is not quenched, and their worm does not die" (Mark 9:44). We further condemn Jewish dreams that there will be a golden age on earth before the Day of Judgment, and that the pious, having subdued all their godless enemies, will possess all the kingdoms of the earth. For evangelical truth in Matt., chs. 24 and 25, and Luke, ch. 18, and apostolic teaching in II Thess., ch. 2, and II Tim., chs. 3 and 4, present something quite different.

THE FRUIT OF CHRIST'S DEATH AND RESURRECTION. Further by his passion and death and everything which he did and endured for our sake by his coming in the flesh, our Lord reconciled all the faithful to the heavenly Father, made expiation for sins, disarmed death, overcame damnation and hell, and by his resurrection from the dead brought again and restored life and immortality. For he is our righteousness, life and resurrection, in a word, the fulness and perfection of all the faithful, salvation and all sufficiency. For the apostle says: "In him all the fulness of God was pleased to dwell," and, "You have come to fulness of life in him" (Col., chs. 1 and 2).

JESUS CHRIST IS THE ONLY SAVIOR OF THE WORLD, AND THE TRUE AWAITED MESSIAH. For we teach and believe that this Jesus Christ our Lord is the unique and eternal Savior of the human race, and thus of the whole world, in whom by faith are saved all who before the law, under the law, and under the Gospel were saved, and however many will be saved at the end of the world. For the Lord himself says in the Gospel: "He who does not enter the sheepfold by the door but climbs in by another way, that man is a thief and a robber....I am the door of the sheep" (John 10:1 and 7). And also in another place in the same Gospel he says: "Abraham saw my day and was glad" (ch. 7:56). The apostle Peter also says: "There is salvation in no one else, for there is no other name under heaven given among men by which we must be saved." We therefore believe that we will be saved through the grace of our Lord Jesus Christ, as our fathers were (Acts 4:12; 10:43; 15:11). For Paul also says: "All our fathers ate the same spiritual food, and all drank the same spiritual drink. For they drank from the spiritual Rock which followed them, and the Rock was Christ" (I Cor. 10:3 f.). And thus we read that John says: "Christ was the Lamb which was slain from the foundation of the world" (Rev. 14:8), and John the Baptist testified that Christ is that "Lamb of God, who takes away the sin of the world" (John 1:29). Wherefore, we quite openly profess and preach that Jesus Christ is the sole Redeemer and Savior of the world, the King and High Priest, the true and awaited Messiah, that holy and blessed one whom all the types of the law and predictions of the prophets prefigured and promised; and that God appointed him beforehand and sent him to us, so that we are not now to look for any other. Now there only remains for all of us to give all glory to Christ, believe in him, rest in him alone, despising and rejecting all other aids in life. For however many seek salvation in any other than in Christ alone, have fallen from the grace of God and have rendered Christ null and void for themselves (Gal. 5:4).

THE CREEDS OF FOUR COUNCILS RECEIVED. And, to say many things with a few words, with a sincere heart we believe, and freely confess with open mouth, whatever things are defined from the Holy Scriptures concerning the mystery of the incarnation of our Lord Jesus Christ, and are summed up in the Creeds and decrees of the first four most excellent synods convened at Nicaea, Constantinople, Ephesus and Chalcedon -- together with the Creed of blessed Athanasius [The so-called Athanasian Creed was not written by Athanasius but dates from the ninth century. It is also called the "Quicunque" from the opening word of the Latin text.], and all similar symbols; and we condemn everything contrary to these.

THE SECTS. And in this way we retain the Christian, orthodox and catholic faith whole and unimpaired; knowing that nothing is contained in the aforesaid symbols which is not agreeable to the Word of God, and does not altogether make for a sincere exposition of the faith.

OF THE LAW OF GOD

THE WILL OF GOD IS EXPLAINED FOR US IN THE LAW OF GOD. We teach that the will of God is explained for us in the law of God, what he wills or does not will us to do, what is good and just, or what is evil and unjust. Therefore, we confess that the law is good and holy.

THE LAW OF NATURE. And this law was at one time written in the hearts of men by the finger of God (Rom. 2:15), and is called the law of nature (the law of Moses is in two Tables), and at another it was inscribed by his finger on the two Tables of Moses, and eloquently expounded in the books of Moses (Ex. 20:1 ff.; Deut. 5:6 ff.). For the sake of clarity we distinguish the moral law which is contained in the Decalogue or two Tables and expounded in the books of Moses, the ceremonial law which determines the ceremonies and worship of God, and the judicial law which is concerned with political and domestic matters.

THE LAW IS COMPLETE AND PERFECT. We believe that the whole will of God and all necessary precepts for every sphere of life are taught in this law. For otherwise the Lord would not have forbidden us to add or to take away anything from this law; neither would he have commanded us to walk in a straight path before this law, and not to turn aside from it by turning to the right or to the left (Deut. 4:2; 12:32).

WHY THE LAW WAS GIVEN. We teach that this law was not given to men that they might be justified by keeping it, but that rather from what it teaches we may know (our) weakness, sin and condemnation, and, despairing of our strength, might be converted to Christ in faith. For the apostle openly declares: "The law brings wrath," and, "Through the law comes knowledge of sin" (Rom. 4:15; 3:20), and, "If a law had been given which could justify or make alive, then righteousness would indeed be by the law. But the Scripture (that is, the law) has concluded all under sin, that the promise which was of the faith of Jesus might be given to those who believe....Therefore, the law was our schoolmaster unto Christ, that we might be justified by faith" (Gal.3:21 ff.).

THE FLESH DOES NOT FULFIL THE LAW. For no flesh could or can satisfy the law of God and fulfil it, because of the weakness in our flesh which adheres and remains in us until our last breath. For the apostle says again: "God has done what the law, weakened by the flesh, could not do: sending his own Son in the likeness of sinful flesh and for sin" (Rom. 8:3). Therefore, Christ is the perfecting of the law and our fulfilment of it (Rom. 10:4), who, in order to take away the curse of the law, was make a curse for us (Gal. 3:13). Thus he imparts to us through faith his fulfilment of the law, and his righteousness and obedience are imputed to us.

HOW FAR THE LAW IS ABROGATED. The law of God is therefore abrogated to the extent that it no longer condemns us, nor works wrath in us. For we are under grace and not under the law. Moreover, Christ has fulfilled all the figures of the law. Hence, with the coming of the body, the shadows ceased, so that in Christ we now have the truth and all fulness. But yet we do not on that account contemptuously reject the law. For we remember the words of the Lord when he said: "I have not come to abolish the law and the prophets but to fulfil them" (Matt. 5:17). We know that in the law is delivered to us the patterns of virtues and vices. We know that the written law when explained by the Gospel is useful to the Church, and that therefore its reading is not to be banished from the Church. For although Moses' face was covered with a veil, yet the apostle says that the veil has been taken away and abolished by Christ.

THE SECTS. We condemn everything that heretics old and new have taught against the law.

OF THE GOSPEL OF JESUS CHRIST, OF THE PROMISES, AND OF THE SPIRIT AND LETTER

THE ANCIENTS HAD EVANGELICAL PROMISES. The Gospel is, indeed, opposed to the law. For the law works wrath and announces a curse, whereas the Gospel preaches grace and blessing. John says: "For the law was given through Moses; grace and truth came through Jesus Christ" (John 1:17). Yet notwithstanding it is most certain that those who were before the law and under the law, were not altogether destitute of the Gospel. For they had extraordinary evangelical promises such as these are: "The seed of the woman shall bruise the serpent's head" (Gen. 3:15). "In thy seed shall all the nations of the earth be blessed" (Gen. 22:18). "The scepter shall not depart from Judah...until he comes" (Gen. 49:10). "The Lord will raise up a prophet from among his own brethren" (Deut. 18:15; Acts 3:22), etc.

THE PROMISES TWOFOLD. And we acknowledge that two kinds of promises were revealed to the fathers, as also to us. For some were of present or earthly things, such as the promises of the Land of Canaan and of victories, and as the promise today still of daily bread. Others were then and are still now of heavenly and eternal things, namely, divine grace, remission of sins, and eternal life through faith in Jesus Christ.

THE FATHERS ALSO HAD NOT ONLY CARNAL BUT SPIRITUAL PROMISES. Moreover, the ancients had not only external and earthly but also spiritual and heavenly promises in Christ. Peter says: "The prophets who prophesied of the grace that was to be yours searched and inquired about this salvation" (I Peter 1:10).

Wherefore the apostle Paul also said: "The Gospel of God was promised beforehand through his prophets in the holy scriptures" (Rom. 1:2). Thereby it is clear that the ancients were not entirely destitute of the whole Gospel.

WHAT IS THE GOSPEL PROPERLY SPEAKING? And although our fathers had the Gospel in this way in the writings of the prophets by which they attained salvation in Christ through faith, yet the Gospel is properly called glad and joyous news, in which, first by John the Baptist, then by Christ the Lord himself, and afterwards by the apostles and their successors, is preached to us in the world that God has now performed what he promised from the beginning of the world, and has sent, nay more, has given us his only Son and in him reconciliation with the Father, the remission of sins, all fulness and everlasting life. Therefore, the history delineated by the four Evangelists and explaining how these things were done or fulfilled by Christ, what things Christ taught and did, and that those who believe in him have all fulness, is rightly called the Gospel. The preaching and writings of the apostles, in which the apostles explain for us how the Son was given to us by the Father, and in him everything that has to do with life and salvation, is also rightly called evangelical doctrine, so that not even today, if sincerely preached, does it lose its illustrious title.

OF THE SPIRIT AND THE LETTER. That same preaching of the Gospel is also called by the apostle "the spirit" and "the ministry of the spirit" because by faith it becomes effectual and living in the ears, nay more, in the hearts of believers through the illumination of the Holy Spirit (II Cor. 3:6). For the letter, which is opposed to the Spirit, signifies everything external, but especially the doctrine of the law which, without the Spirit and faith, works wrath and provokes sin in the minds of those who do not have a living faith. For this reason the apostle calls it "the ministry of death." In this connection the saying of the apostle is pertinent: "The letter kills, but the Spirit gives life." And false apostles preached a corrupted Gospel, having combined it with the law, as if Christ could not save without the law.

THE SECTS. Such were the Ebionites said to be, who were descended from Ebion the heretic, and the Nazarites who were formerly called Mineans. All these we condemn, while preaching the pure Gospel and teaching that believers are justified by the Spirit [The original manuscript has "Christ" instead of "Spirit".] alone, and not by the law. A more detailed exposition of this matter will follow presently under the heading of justification.

THE TEACHING OF THE GOSPEL IS NOT NEW, BUT MOST ANCIENT DOCTRINE. And although the teaching of the Gospel, compared with the teaching of the Pharisees concerning the law, seemed to be a new doctrine when first preached by Christ (which Jeremiah also prophesied concerning the New Teatament), yet actually it not only was and still is an old doctrine (even if today it is called new by the Papists when compared with the teaching now received among them), but is the most ancient of all in the world. For God predestinated from eternity to save the world through Christ, and he has disclosed to the world through the Gospel this his predestination and eternal counsel (II Tim. 2:9 f.). Hence it is evident that the religion and teaching of the Gospel among all who ever were, are and will be, is the most ancient of all. Wherefore we assert that all who say that the religion and teaching of the Gospel is a faith which has recently arisen, being scarcely thirty years old, err disgracefully and speak shamefully of the eternal counsel of God. To them applies the saying of Isaiah the prophet: "Woe to those who call evil good and good evil, who put darkness for light and light for darkness, who put bitter for sweet and sweet for bitter!" (Isa. 5:20).

OF REPENTANCE AND THE CONVERSION OF MAN

THE doctrine of repentance is joined with the Gospel. For so has the Lord said in the Gospel: "Repentance and forgiveness of sins should be preached in my name to all nations" (Luke 24:47).

WHAT IS REPENTANCE? By repentance we understand (1) the recovery of a right mind in sinful man awakened by the Word of the Gospel and the Holy Spirit, and received by true faith, by which the sinner immediately acknowledges his innate corruption and all his sins accused by the Word of God; and (2) grieves for them from his heart, and not only bewails and frankly confesses them before God with a feeling of shame, but also (3) with indignation abominates them; and (4) now zealously considers the amendment of his ways and constantly strives for innocence and virtue in which conscientiously to exercise himself all the rest of his life.

TRUE REPENTANCE IS CONVERSION TO GOD. And this is true repentance, namely, a sincere turning to God and all good, and earnest turning away from the devil and all evil.

1. REPENTANCE IS A GIFT OF GOD. Now we expressly say that this repentance is a sheer gift of God and not a work of our strength. For the apostle commands a faithful minister diligently to instruct those who oppose the truth, if "God may perhaps grant that they will repent and come to know the truth" (II Tim. 2:25).

2. LAMENTS SINS COMMITTED. Now that sinful woman who washed the feet of the Lord with her tears, and Peter who wept bitterly and bewailed his denial of the Lord (Luke 7:38; 22:62) show clearly how the mind of a penitent man ought to be seriously lamenting the sins he has committed.

3. CONFESSES SINS TO GOD. Moreover, the prodigal son and the publican in the Gospel, when compared with the Pharisee, present us with the most suitable pattern of how our sins are to be confessed to God. The former said: "Father, I have sinned against heaven and before you; I am no longer worthy to be called your son; treat me as one of your hired servants" (Luke 15:8 ff.). And the latter, not daring to raise his eyes to heaven, beat his breast, saying, "God be merciful to me a sinner" (ch. 18:13). And we do not doubt that they were accepted by God into grace. For the apostle John says: "If we confess our sins, he is faithful and just, and will forgive our sins and cleanse us from all unrighteousness. If we say we have not sinned, we make him a liar, and his word is not in us" (I John 1:9 f.).

SACERDOTAL CONFESSION AND ABSOLUTION. But we believe that this sincere confession which is made to God alone, either privately between God and the sinner, or publicly in the Church where the general confession of sins is said, is sufficient, and that in order to obtain forgiveness of sins it is not necessary for anyone to confess his sins to a priest, mumuring them in his ears, that in turn he might receive absolution from the priest with his laying on of hands, because there is neither a commandment nor an example of this in Holy Scriptures. David testifies and says: "I acknowledged my sin to thee, and did not hide my iniquity; I said, `I will confess my transgressions to the Lord'; then thou didst forgive the guilt of my sin" (Ps. 32:5). And the Lord who taught us to pray and at the same time to confess our sins said: "Pray then like this: Our Father, who art in heaven,...forgive us our debts, as we also forgive our debtors"

(Matt. 6:12). Therefore it is necessary that we confess our sins to God our Father, and be reconciled with our neighbor if we have offended him. Concerning this kind of confession, the Apostle James says: "Confess your sins to one another" (James 5:16). If, however, anyone is overwhelmed by the burden of his sins and by perplexing temptations, and will seek counsel, instruction and comfort privately, either from a minister of the Church, or from any other brother who is instructed in God's law, we do not disapprove; just as we also fully approve of that general and public confession of sins which is usually said in Church and in meetings for worship, as we noted above, inasmuch as it is agreeable to Scripture.

OF THE KEYS OF THE KINGDOM OF HEAVEN. Concerning the keys of the Kingdom of Heaven which the Lord gave to the apostles, many babble many astonishing things, and out of them forge swords, spears, scepters and crowns, and complete power over the greatest kingdoms, indeed, over souls and bodies. Judging simply according to the Word of the Lord, we say that all properly called ministers possess and exercise the keys or the use of them when they proclaim the Gospel; that is, when they teach, exhort, comfort, rebuke, and keep in discipline the people committed to their trust.

OPENING AND SHUTTING (THE KINGDOM). For in this way they open the Kingdom of Heaven to the obedient and shut it to the disobedient. The Lord promised these keys to the apostles in Matt., ch. 16, and gave them in John, ch. 20, Mark, ch. 16, and Luke, ch. 24, when he sent out his disciples and commanded them to preach the Gospel in all the world, and to remit sins.

THE MINISTRY OF RECONCILIATION. In the letter to the Corinthians the apostle says that the Lord gave the ministry of reconciliation to his ministers (II Cor. 5:18 ff.). And what this is he then explains, saying that it is the preaching or teaching of reconciliation. And explaining his words still more clearly he adds that Christ's ministers discharge the office of an ambassador in Christ's name, as if God himself through ministers exhorted the people to be reconciled to God, doubtless by faithful obedience. Therefore, they excercise the keys when they persuade [men] to believe and repent. Thus they reconcile men to God.

MINISTERS REMIT SINS. Thus they remit sins. Thus they open the Kingdom of Heaven, and bring believers into it: very different from those of whom the Lord said in the Gospel, "Woe to you lawyers! For you have taken away the key of knowledge; you did not enter yourselves, and you hindered those who were entering."

HOW MINISTERS ABSOLVE. Ministers, therefore, rightly and effectually absolve when they preach the Gospel of Christ and thereby the remission of sins, which is promised to each one who believes, just as each one is baptized, and when they testify that it pertains to each one peculiarly. Neither do we think that this absolution becomes more effectual by being murmured in the ear of someone or by being murmured singly over someone's head. We are nevertheless of the opinion that the remission of sins in the blood of Christ is to be diligently proclaimed, and that each one is to be admonished that the forgiveness of sins pertains to him.

DILIGENCE IN THE RENEWAL OF LIFE. But the examples in the Gospel teach us how vigilant and diligent the penitent ought to be in striving for newness of life and in mortifying the old man and quickening the new. For the Lord said to the man he healed of palsy: "See, you are well! Sin no more, that nothing worse befall you" (John 5:14). Likewise to the adulteress whom he set free he said: "Go, and sin no more" (ch. 8:11). To be sure, by these words he did not mean that any man, as long as he lived in the flesh, could not sin; he simply recommends diligence and a careful devotion, so that we should strive by all means, and beseech God in prayers lest we fall back into sins from which, as it were, we have been resurrected, and lest we be overcome by the flesh, the world and the devil. Zacchaeus the publican, whom the Lord had received back into favor, exclaims in the Gospel: "Behold, Lord, the half of my goods I give to the poor; and if I have defrauded any one of anything, I restore it fourfold" (Luke 19:8). Therefore, in the same way we preach that restitution and compassion, and even almsgiving, are necessary for those who truly repent, and we exhort all men everywhere in the words of the apostle: "Let not sin therefore reign in your mortal bodies, to make you obey their passions. Do not yield your members to sin as instruments of wickedness, but yield yourselves to God as men who have been brought from death to life, and your members to God as instruments of righteousness" (Rom. 6:12 f.).

ERRORS. Wherefore we condemn all impious utterances of some who wrongly use the preaching of the Gospel and say that it is easy to return to God. Christ has atoned for all sins. Forgiveness of sins is easy. Therefore, what harm is there in sinning? Nor need we be greatly concerned about repentance, etc. Notwithstanding we always teach that an access to God is open to all sinners, and that he forgives all sinners of all sins except the one sin against the Holy Spirit (Mark 3:29).

THE SECTS. Wherefore we condemn both old and new Novatians and Catharists.

PAPAL INDULGENCES. We especially condemn the lucrative doctrine of the Pope concerning penance, and against his simony and his simoniacal indulgences we avail ourselves of

Peter's judgment concerning Simon: "Your silver perish with you, because you thought you could obtain the gift of God with money! You have neither part nor lot in this matter, for your heart is not right before God" (Acts 8:20 f.).

SATISFACTIONS. We also disapprove of those who think that by their own satisfactions they make amends for sins committed. For we teach that Christ alone by his death or passion is the satisfaction, propitiation or expiation of all sins (Isa., ch.53; I Cor. 1:30). Yet as we have already said, we do not cease to urge the mortification of the flesh. We add, however, that this mortification is not to be proudly obtruded upon God as a satisfaction for sins, but is to be performed humble, in keeping with the nature of the children of God, as a new obedience out of gratitude for the deliverance and full satisfaction obtained by the death and satisfaction of the Son of God.

OF THE TRUE JUSTIFICATION OF THE FAITHFUL

WHAT IS JUSTIFICATION? According to the apostle in his treatment of justification, to justify means to remit sins, to absolve from guilt and punishment, to receive into favor, and to pronounce a man just. For in his epistle to the Romans the apostle says: "It is God who justifies; who is to condemn?" (Rom. 8:33). To justify and to condemn are opposed. And in The Acts of the Apostles the apostle states: "Through Christ forgiveness of sins is proclaimed to you, and by him everyone that believes is freed from everything from which you could not be freed by the law of Moses" (Acts 13:38 f.). For in the Law and also in the Prophets we read: "If there is a dispute between men, and they come into court...the judges decide between them, acquitting the innocent and condemning the guilty" (Deut. 25:1). And in Isa., ch. 5: "Woe to those...who aqcuit the guilty for a bribe."

WE ARE JUSTIFIED ON ACCOUNT OF CHRIST. Now it is most certain that all of us are by nature sinners and godless, and before God's judgment-seat are convicted of godlessness and are guilty of death, but that, solely by the grace of Christ and not from any merit of ours or consideration for us, we are justified, that is, absolved from sin and death by God the Judge. For what is clearer than what Paul said: "Since all have sinned and fall short of the glory of God, they are justified by his grace as a gift, through the redemption which is in Christ Jesus" (Rom. 3:23 f.).

IMPUTED RIGHTEOUSNESS. For Christ took upon himself and bore the sins of the world, and satisfied divine justice. Therefore, solely on account of Christ's sufferings and resurrection God is propitious with respect to our sins and does not impute them to us, but imputes Christ's righteousness to us as our own (II Cor. 5;19 ff.; Rom. 4;25), so that now we are not only cleansed and purged from sins or are holy, but also, granted the righteousness of Christ, and so absolved from sin, death and condemnation, are at last righteous and heirs of eternal life. Properly speaking, therefore, God alone justifies us, and justifies only on account of Christ, not imputing sins to us but imputing his righteousness to us.

WE ARE JUSFIFIED BY FAITH ALONE. But because we receive this justification, not through any works, but through faith in the mercy of God and in Christ, we therefore teach and believe with the apostle that sinful man is justified by faith alone in Christ, not by the law or any works. For the apostle says: "We hold that a man is justified by faith apart from works of law" (Rom. 3:28). Also: "If Abraham was justified by works, he has something to boast about, but not before God. For what does the scripture say? Abraham believed God, and it was reckoned to him as righteousness....And to one who does not work but believes in him who justifies the ungodly, his faith is reckoned as righteousness" (Rom. 4:2 ff.; Gen. 15:6). And again: "By grace you have been saved through faith; and this is not your own doing, it is the gift of God--not because of works, lest any man should boast," etc. (Eph. 2:8 f.). Therefore, because faith receives Christ our righteousness and attributes everything to the grace of God in Christ, on that account justification is attributed to faith, chiefly because of Christ and not therefore because it is our work. For it is the gift of God.

WE RECEIVE CHRIST BY FAITH. Moreover, the Lord abundantly shows that we receive Christ by faith, in John, ch. 6, where he puts eating for believing, and believing for eating. For as we receive food by eating, so we participate in Christ by believing.

JUSTIFICATION IS NOT ATTRIBUTED PARTLY TO CHRIST OR TO FAITH, PARTLY TO US. Therefore, we do not share in the benefit of justification partly because of the grace of God or Christ, and partly because of ourselves, our love, works or merit, but we attribute it wholly to the grace of God in Christ through faith. For our love and our works could not please God in Christ through faith. For our love and our works could not please God if performed by unrighteous men. Therefore, it is necessary for us to be righteous before we may love and do good works. We are made trulyrighteous, as we have said, by faith in Christ purely by the grace of God, who does not impute to us our sins, but the righteousness of Christ, or rather, he imputes faith in Christ to us for righteousness. Moreover, the apostle very clearly derives love from faith when he says: "The aim of our command is love that issues from a pure heart, a good conscience, and a sincere faith" (I Tim. 1:5)

JAMES COMPARED WITH PAUL. Wherefore, in this matter we are not speaking of a fictitious, empty, lazy and dead faith, but of a living, quickening faith. It is and is called a living faith because it apprehends Christ who is life and makes alive, and shows that it is alive by living works. And so James does not contradict anything in this doctrine of ours. For he speaks of an empty, dead faith of which some boasted but who did not have Christ living in them by faith (James 2:14 ff.). James said that works justify, yet without contradicting the apostle (otherwise he would have to be rejected) but showing that Abraham proved his living and justifying faith by works. This all the pious do, but they trust in Christ alone and not in their own works. For again the apostle said: "It is no longer I who live, but Christ who lives in me; and the life I now live in the flesh I live by faith in the Son of God, [The Latin reads: "by the faith of the Son of God."] who loved me and gave himself for me. I do not reject the grace of God; for if justification were through the law, then Christ died to no purpose," etc. (Gal. 2:20 f.).

OF FAITH AND GOOD WORKS, AND OF THEIR REWARD, AND OF MAN'S MERIT

WHAT IS FAITH? Christian faith is not an opinion or human conviction, but a most firm trust and a clear and steadfast assent of the mind, and then a most certain apprehension of the truth of God presented in the Scriptures and in the Apostles' Creed, and thus also of God himself, the greatest good, and especially of God's promise and of Christ who is the fulfilment of all promises.

FAITH IS THE GIFT OF GOD. But this faith is a pure gift of God which God alone of his grace gives to his elect according to this measure when, to whom and to the degree he wills. And he does this by the holy Spirit by means of the preaching of the Gospel and steadfast prayer.

THE INCREASE OF FAITH. This faith also has its increase, and unless it were given by God, the apostles would not have said: "Lord, increase our faith" (Luke 17:5). And all these things which up to this point we have said concerning faith, the apostles have taught before us. For Paul said: "For faith is the sure subsistence, of things hoped for, and the clear and certain apprehension" (Heb. 11:1). And again he says that all the promises of God are Yes through Christ and through Christ are Amen (II Cor. 1:20). And to the Philippians he said that it has been given tothem to believe in Christ (Phil. 1:29). Again, God assigned to each the measure of faith (Rom. 12:3). Again: "Not all have faith" and, "Not all obey the Gospel" (II Thess. 3:2; Rom. 10:16). But Luke also bears witness, saying: "As many as were ordained to life believed" (Acts 13:48). Wherefore Paul also calls faith "the faith of God's elect" (Titus 1:1), and again: "Faith comes from hearing, and hearing comes by the Word of God" (Rom. 10:17). Elsewhere he often commands men to pray for faith.

FAITH EFFICACIOUS AND ACTIVE. The same apostle calls faith efficacious and active through love (Gal. 5:6). It also quiets the conscience and opens a free access to God, so that we may draw near to him with confidence and may obtain from him what is useful and necessary. The same [faith] keeps us in the service we owe to God and our neighbor, strengthens our patience in adversity, fashions and makes a true confession, and in a word brings forth good fruit of all kinds, and good works.

CONCERNING GOOD WORKS. For we teach that truly good works grow out of a living faith by the Holy Spirit and are done by the faithful according tothe will or rule of God's Word. Now the apostle Peter says: "Make every effort to supplement your faith with virtue, and virtue with knowledge, and knowledge with self-control," etc.(II Peter 1:5 ff.). But we have said above that the law of God, which is his will, prescribes for us the pattern of good works. And the apostle says: "This is the will of God, your sanctification, that you abstain form immorality...that no man transgress, and wrong his brother in business" (I Thess. 4:3 ff.).

WORKS OF HUMAN CHOICE. And indeed works and worship which we choose arbitrarily are not pleasing to God. These Paul calls "self-devised worship" Col. 2:23. Of such the Lord says in the Gospel: "In vain do they worship me, teaching as doctrines the precepts of men" (Matt. 15:9). Therefore, we disapprove of such works, and approve and urge those that are of God's will and commission.

THE END OF GOOD WORKS. These same works ought not to be done in order that we may earn eternal life by them, for, as the apostle says, eternal life is the gift of God. Nor are they to be done for ostentation which the Lord rejects in Matt., ch. 6, nor for gain which he also rejects in Matt., ch. 23, but for the glory of God, to adorn our calling, to show gratitude to God, and for the profit of the neighbor. For our Lord says again in the Gospel: "Let your light so shine before men, that they may see your good works and give glory to your Father who is in heaven" (Matt. 5:16). And the apostle Paul says: "Lead a life worthy of the calling to which you have been called" (Eph. 4:1). Also: "And whatever you do, in word or deed, do everything in the name of the Lord Jesus, giving thanks to God and to the Fatehr through him" (Col. 3:17), and, "Let each of you look not to his own interests, but to the interests of others" (Phil. 2:4), and, "Let our people learn to apply themselves to good deeds, so as to help cases of urgent need, and not to be unfruitful" (Titus 3;14).

GOOD WORKS NOT REJECTED. Therefore, although we teach with the apostle that a man is justified by grace through faith in Christ and not through any good works, yet we do not think that good works are of little value and condemn them. We know that man was not created or regenerated through faith in order to be idle, but rather that without ceasing he should do those things which are good and useful. For in the Gospel the Lord says that a good tree brings forth good fruit (Matt. 12:33), and that he who abides in me bears much fruit (John 15:5). The apostle says: "For we are his workmanship, created in Christ Jesus for good works, which God prepared beforehand, that we should walk in them" (Eph. 2:10), and again: "Who gave himself for us to redeem us from all iniquity and to purify for himself a people of his own who are zealous for good deeds" (Titus 2:14). We therefore condemn all who despise good works and who babble that they are useless and that we do not need to pay attention to them.

WE ARE NOT SAVED BY GOOD WORKS. Nevertheless, as was said above, we do not think that we are saved by good works, and that they are so necessary for salvation that no one was ever saved without them. For we are saved by grace and the favor of Christ alone. Works necessarily proceed from faith. And salvation is improperly attributed to them, but is most properly ascribed to grace. The apostle's sentence is well known: "If it is by grace, then it is no longer of works; otherwise grace would no longer be grace. But if it is of works, then it is no longer grace, because otherwise work is no longer work" (Rom. 11:6).

GOOD WORKS PLEASE GOD. Now the works which we do by faith are pleasing to God and are approved by him. Because of faith in Christ, those who do good works which, moreover, are done from God's grace through the Holy Spirit, are pleasing to god. For St. Peter said: "In every nation anyone who fears God and does what is right is acceptable to him" (Acts 10:35). And Paul said: "We have not ceased to pray for you...that you may walk worthily of the Lord, fully pleasing to him, bearing fruit in every good work" (Col. 1:9 f.).

WE TEACH TRUE, NOT FALSE AND PHILOSOPHICAL VIRTUES. And so we diligently teach true, not false and philosophical virtues, truly good works, and the genuine service of a Christian. And as much as we can we diligently and zealously press them upon all men, while censuring the sloth and Hypocrisy of all those who praise and profess the Gospel with their lips and dishonor it by their disgraceful lives. In this matter we place before them God's terrible threats and then his rich promises and generous rewards -- exhorting, consoling and rebuking.

GOD GIVES A REWARD FOR GOOD WORKS. For we teach that God gives a rich reward to those who do good works, according to that saying of the prophet: "keep your voice from weeping,...for your work shall be rewarded" (Jer. 31:16; Isa., ch. 4).

The Lord also said in the Gospel: "Rejoice and be glad, for your reward is great in heaven" (Matt. 5:12), and, "Whoever gives to one of these my little ones a cup of cold water, truly, I say to you, he shall not lose his reward" (ch. 10:42). However, we do not ascribe this reward, which the Lord gives, to the merit of the man who receives it, but to the goodness, generosity and truthfulness of God who promises and gives it, and who, although he owes nothing to anyone, nevertheless promises that he will give a reward to his faithful worshippers; meanwhile he also gives them that they may honor him. Moreover, in the works even of the saints there is much that is unworthy of God and very much that is imperfect. But because God receives into favor and embraces those who do works for Christ's sake, he grants to them the promised reward. For in other respects our righteousnesses are compared to a filthy wrap (Isa. 64:6). And the Lord says in the Gospel: "When you have done all that is commanded you, say, "We are unworthy servants; we have only done what was our duty" (Like 17:10).

THERE ARE NO MERITS OF MEN. Therefore, although we teach that God rewards our good deeds, yet at the same time we teach, with Augustine, that God does not crown in us our merits but his gifts. Accordingly we say that whatever reward we receive is also grace, and is more grace than reward, because the good we do, we do more through God than through ourselves, and because Paul says: "What have you that you did not receive? If then you received it, why do you boast as if you had not received it?" (I Cor. 4:7). And this is what the blessed martyr Cyprian concluded from this verse: We are not to glory in anything in us, since nothing is our own. We therefore condemn those who defend the merits of men in such a way that they invalidate the grace of God.

OF THE CATHOLIC AND HOLY CHURCH OF GOD, AND OF THE ONE ONLY HEAD OF THE CHURCH

THE CHURCH HAS ALWAYS EXISTED AND IT WILL ALWAYS EXIST. But because God from the beginning would have men to be saved, and to come to the knowledge of the truth (I Tim. 2:4), it is altogether necessary that there always should have been, and should be now, and to the end of the world, a Church.

WHAT IS THE CHURCH? The Church is an assembly of the faithful called or gathered out of the world; a communion, I say, of all saints, namely, of those who truly know and rightly worship and serve the true God in Christ the Savior, by the Word and holy Spirit, and who by faith are partakers of all benefits which are freely offered through Christ.

CITIZENS OF ONE COMMONWEALTH. They are all citizens of the one city, living under the same Lord, under the same laws and in the same fellowship of all good things. For the apostle calls them "fellow citizens with the saints and members of the household of God" (Eph. 2:19), calling the faithful on earth saints (I Cor. 4:1), who are sanctified by the blood of the Son of God. The article of the Creed, "I believe in the holy catholic Church, the communion of saints," is to be understood wholly as concerning these saints.

ONLY ONE CHURCH FOR ALL TIMES. And since there is always but one God, and there is one mediator between God and men, Jesus the Messiah, and one Shepherd of the whole flock, one

Head of this body, and, to conclude, one Spirit, one salvation, one faith, one Testament or covenant, it necessarily follows that there is only one Church.

THE CATHOLIC CHURCH. We, therefore, call this Church catholic because it is universal, scattered through all parts of the world, and extended unto all times, and is not limited to any times or places. Therefore, we condemn the Donatists who confined the Church to I know not what corners of Africa. Nor do we approve of the Roman clergy who have recently passed off only the Roman Church as catholic.

PARTS OR FORMS OF THE CHURCH. The Church is divided into different parts or forms; not because it is divided or rent asunder in itself, but rather because it is distinguished by the diversity of the numbers that are in it.

MILITANT AND TRIUMPHANT. For the one is called the Church Militant, the other the Church Triumphant. The former still wages war on earth, and fights against the flesh, the world, and the prince of this world, the devil; against sin and death. But the latter, having been now discharged, triumphs in heaven immediately after having overcome all those things and rejoices before the Lord. Notwithstanding both have fellowship and union one with another.

THE PARTICULAR CHURCH. Moreover, the Church Militant upon the earth has always had many particular churches. yet all these are to be referred to the unity of the catholic Church. This [Militant] Church was set up differently before the Law among the patriarchs; otherwise under Moses by the Law; and differently by Christ through the Gospel.

THE TWO PEOPLES. Generally two peoples are usually counted, namely, the Israelites and Gentiles, or those who have been gathered from among Jews and Gentiles into the Church. There are also two Testaments, the Old and the New.

THE SAME CHURCH FOR THE OLD AND THE NEW PEOPLE. Yet from all these people there was and is one fellowship, one salvation in the one Messiah; in whom, as members of one body under one Head, all united together in the same faith, partaking also of the same spiritual food and drink. Yet here we acknowledge a diversity of times, and a diversity in the signs of the promised and delivered Christ; and that now the ceremonies being abolished, the light shines unto us more clearly, and blessings are given to us more abundantly, and a fuller liberty.

THE CHURCH THE TEMPLE OF THE LIVING GOD. This holy Church of God is called the temple of the living God, built of living and spiritual stones and founded upon a firm rock, upon a foundation which no other can lay, and therefore it is called "the pillar and bulwark of the truth" (I Tim. 3:15).

THE CHURCH DOES NOT ERR. It does not err as long as it rests upon the rock Christ, and upon the foundation of the prophets and apostles. And it is no wonder if it errs, as often as it deserts him who alone is the truth.

THE CHURCH AS BRIDE AND VIRGIN. This Church is also called a virgin and the Bride of Christ, and even the only Beloved. For the apostle says: "I betrothed you to Christ to present you as a pure bride to Christ" (II Cor. 11:2).

THE CHURCH AS A FLOCK OF SHEEP. The Church is called a flock of sheep under the one shepherd, Christ, according to Ezek., ch. 34, and John, ch. 10.

THE CHURCH AS THE BODY. It is also called the body of Christ because the faithful are living members of Christ under Christ the Head.

CHRIST THE SOLE HEAD OF THE CHURCH. It is the head which has the preeminence in the body, and from it the whole body receives life; by its spirit the body is governed in all things; from it, also, the body receives increase, that it may grow up. Also, there is one head of the body, and it is suited to the body. Therefore the Church cannot have any other head besides Christ. For as the Church is a spiritual body, so it must also have a spiritual head in harmony with itself. Neither can it be governed by any other spirit than by the Spirit of Christ. Wherefore Paul says: "He is the head of the body, the church; he is the beginning, the firstborn from the dead, that in everything he might be preeminent" (Col. 1:18). And in another place: "Christ is the head of the church, his body, and is himself its Savior" (Eph. 5:23). And again: he is "the head over all things for the church, which is his body, the fulness of him who fills all in all" (Eph. 1:22 f.). Also: "We are to grow up in every way into him who is the head, into Christ, from whom the whole body, joined and knit together, makes bodily growth" (Eph. 4:15 f.). And therefore we do not approve of the doctrine of the Roman clergy, who make their Pope at Rome the universal shepherd and supreme head of the Church Militant here on earth, and so the very vicar of Jesus Christ, who has (as they say) all fulness of power and sovereign authority in the Church.

CHRIST THE ONLY PASTOR OF THE CHURCH. For we teach that Christ the Lord is, and remains the only universal pastor, and highest Pontiff before God the Father; and that in the Church he himself performs all the duties of a bishop or pastor, even to the world's end; [Vicar] and therefore does not need a substitute for one who is absent. For Christ is present with his Church, and is its life-giving Head.

NO PRIMACY IN THE CHURCH. He has strictly forbidden his apostles and their successors to have any primacy and dominion in the Church. Who does not see, therefore, that whoever contradicts and opposes this plain truth is rather to be counted among the number of those of whom Christ's apostles prophesied: Peter in II Peter, ch. 2, and Paul in Acts 20:2; II Cor. 11:2; II Thess., ch.2, and also in other places?

NO DISORDER IN THE CHURCH. However, by doing away with a Roman head we do not bring any confusion or disorder into the Church, since we teach that the government of the Church which the apostles handed down is sufficient to keep the Church in proper order, the Church was not disordered or in confusion. The Roman head does indeed preserve his tyranny and the corruption that has been brought into the Church, and meanwhile he hinders, resists, and with all the strength he can muster cuts off the proper reformation of the Church.

DISSENSIONS AND STRIFE IN THE CHURCH. We are reproached because there have been manifold dissensions and strife in our churches since they separated themselves from the Church of Rome, and therefore cannot be true churches. As though there were never in the Church of Rome any sects, nor contentions and quarrels concerning religion, and indeed, carried on not so much in the schools as from pulpits in the midst of the people. We know, to be sure, that the apostle said: "God is not a God of confusion but of peace" (I Cor. 14:33), and, "While there is jealousy and strife among you, are you not of the flesh?" Yet we cannot deny that God was in the apostolic Church and that it was a true Church, even though there were wranglings and dissensions in it. The apostle Paul reprehended Peter, an apostle (Gal. 2:11 ff.), and Barnabas dissented from Paul. Great contention arose in the Church of Antioch between them that preached the one Christ, as Luke records in The Acts of the Apostles, ch. 15. And there have at all times been great contentions in the Church, and the most excellent teachers of the Church have differed among themselves about important matters without meanwhile the Church ceasing to be the Church because of these contentions. For thus it pleases God to use the dissensions that arise in the Church to the glory of his name, to illustrate the truth, and in order that those who are in the right might be manifest (I Cor. 11:19).

OF THE NOTES OR SIGNS OF THE TRUE CHURCH. Moreover, as we acknowledge no other head of the Church than Christ, so we do not acknowledge every church to be the true Church which vaunts herself to be such; but we teach that the true Church is that in which the signs or marks of the true Church are to be found, especially the lawful and sincere preaching of the Word of God as it was delivered to us in the books of the prophets and the apostles, which all lead us unto Christ, who said in the Gospel: "My sheep hear me voice, and I know them, and they follow me; and I give unto them eternal life. A stranger they do not follow, but they flee from him, for they do not know the voice of strangers" (John 10:5, 27, 28).

And those who are such in the Church have one faith and one spirit; and therefore they worship but one God, and him alone they worship in spirit and in truth, loving him alone with all their hearts and with all their strength, praying unto him alone through Jesus Christ, the only Mediator and Intercessor; and they do not seek righteousness and life outside Christ and faith in him. Because they acknowledge Christ the only head and foundation of the Church, and, resting on him, daily renew themselves by repentance, and patiently bear the cross laid upon them. Moreover, joined together with all the members of

Christ by an unfeigned love, they show that they are Christ's disciples by persevering in the bond of peace and holy unity. At the same time they participate in the sacraments instituted by Christ, and delivered unto us by his apostles, using them in no other way than as they received them from the Lord. That saying of the apostle Paul is well known to all: "I received from the Lord what I also delivered to you" (I Cor. 11:23 ff.). Accordingly, we condemn all such churches as strangers from the true Church of Christ, which are not such as we have heard they ought to be, no matter how much they brag of a succession of bishops, of unity, and of antiquity. Moreover, we have a charge from the apostles of Christ "ti shun the worship of idols" (I Cor. 10:14; I John 5:21), and "to come out of Babylon," and to have no fellowship with her, unless we want to be partakers with her of all God's plagues (Rev. 18:4; II Cor. 6:17).

OUTSIDE THE CHURCH OF GOD THERE IS NO SALVATION. But we esteem fellowship with the true Church of Christ so highly that we deny that those can live before God who do not stand in fellowship with the true Church of God, but separate themselves from it. For as there was no salvation outside Noah's ark when the world perished in flood; so we believe that there is no certain salvation outside Christ, who offers himself to be enjoyed by the elect in the Church; and hence we teach that those who wish to live ought not to be separated from the true Church of Christ.

THE CHURCH IS NOT BOUND TO ITS SIGNS. Nevertheless, by the signs [of the true Church] mentioned above, we do not so narrowly restrict the Church as to teach that all those are outside the Church who either do not participate in the sacraments, at least not willingly and through contempt, but rather, being forced by necessity, unwillingly abstain from them or are deprived of them; or in whom faith sometimes fails, though it is not entirely extinguished and does not wholly cease;

or in whom imperfections and errors due to weakness are found. For we know that God had some friends in the world outside the commonwealth of Israel. We know what befell the people of God in the captivity of Babylon, where they were deprived of their sacrifices for seventy years. We know what happened to St. Peter, who denied his Master, and what is wont to happen daily to God's elect and faithful people who go astray and are weak. We know, moreover, what kind of churches the churches in Galatia and Corinth were in the apostles' time, in which the apostle found fault with many serious offenses; yet he calls them holy churches of Christ (I Cor. 1:2; Gal. 1:2).

THE CHURCH APPEARS AT TIMES TO BE EXTINCT. Yes, and it sometimes happens that God in his just judgment allows the truth of his Word, and the catholic faith, and the proper worship of God to be so obscured and overthrown that the Church seems almost extinct, and no more to exist, as we see to have happened in the days of Elijah (I Kings 19:10, 14), and at other times. Meanwhile God has in this world and in this darkness his true worshippers, and those not a few, but even seven thousand and more (I Kings 19:18; Rev. 7:3 ff.). For the apostle exclaims: "God's firm foundation stands, bearing this seal, `The Lord knows those who are his,' " etc. (II Tim. 2:19). Whence the Church of God may be termed invisible; not because the men from whom the Church is gathered are invisible, but because, being hidden from our eyes and known only to God, it often secretly escapes human judgment.

NOT ALL WHO ARE IN THE CHURCH ARE OF THE CHURCH. Again, not all that are reckoned in the number of the Church are saints, and living and true members of the Church. For there are many hypocrites, who outwardly hear the Word of God, and publicly receive the sacraments, and seem to pray to God through Christ alone, to confess Christ to be their only righteousness, and to worship God, and to exercise the duties of charity, and for a time to endure with patience in misfortune. And yet they are inwardly destitute of true illumination of the Spirit, of faith and sincerity of heart, and of perseverance to the end. But eventually the character of these men, for the most part, will be disclosed. For the apostle John says: "They went out from us, but they were not of us; for if they had been of us, they would indeed have continued with us" (I John 2:19). And although while they simulate piety they are not of the Church, yet they are considered to be in the Church, just as traitors in a state are numbered among its citizens before they are discovered; and as the tares or darnel and chaff are found among the wheat, and as swellings and tumors are found in a sound body, And therefore the Church of God is rightly compared to a net which catches fish of all kinds, and to a field, in which both wheat and tares are found (Matt. 13:24 ff., 47 ff.).

WE MUST NOT JUDGE RASHLY OR PREMATURELY. Hence we must be very careful not to judge before the time, nor undertake to exclude, reject or cut off those whom the Lord does not want to have excluded or rejected, and those whom we cannot eliminate without loss to the Church. On the other hand, we must be vigilant lest while the pious snore the wicked gain ground and do harm to the Church.

THE UNITY OF THE CHURCH IS NOT IN EXTERNAL RITES. Furthermore, we diligently teach that care is to be taken wherein the truth and unity of the Church chiefly lies, lest we rashly provoke and foster schisms in the Church. Unity consists not in outward rites and ceremonies, but rather in the truth and unity of the catholic faith. The catholic faith is not given to us by human laws, but by Holy Scriptures, of which the Apostles' Creed is a compendium. And, therefore, we read in the ancient writers that there was a manifold diversity of rites, but that they were free, and no one ever thought that the unity of the Church was thereby dissolved. So we teach that the true harmony of the Church consists in doctrines and in the true and harmonious preaching of the Gospel of Christ, and in rites that have been expressly delivered by the Lord. And here we especially urge that saying of the apostle: "Let those of us who are perfect have this mind; and if in any thing you are otherwise minded, God will reveal that also to you. Nevertheless let us walk by the same rule according to what we have attained, and let us be of the same mind" (Phil. 3:15 f.).

OF THE MINISTERS OF THE CHURCH, THEIR INSTITUTION AND DUTIES

GOD USES MINISTERS IN THE BUILDING OF THE CHURCH. God has always used ministers for the gathering or establishing of a Church for himself, and for the governing and preservation of the same; and still he does, and always will, use them so long as the Church remains on earth. Therefore, the first beginning, institution, and office of ministers is a most ancient arrangement of God himself, and not a new one of men.

INSTITUTION AND ORIGIN OF MINISTERS. It is true that God can, by his power, without any means join to himself a Church from among men; but he preferred to deal with men by the ministry of men. Therefore ministers are to be regarded, not as ministers by themselves alone, but as the ministers of God, inasmuch as God effects the salvation of men through them.

THE MINISTRY IS NOT TO BE DESPISED. Hence we warn men to beware lest we attribute what has to do with our conversion and instruction to the secret power of the Holy Spirit in such a way that we make void the ecclesiastical ministry. For it is fitting that we always have in mind the words of the apostle: "How are they to believe in him of whom they have not heard? And how are they to hear without a preacher? So faith comes from hearing, and hearing comes by the word of God" (Rom. 10: 14, 17). And also what the Lord said in the Gospel: "Truly, truly, I say to you, he who receives any one whom I send receives me; and he who receives me receives him who sent me" (John 13:20). Likewise a man of Macedonia, who appeared to Paul in a vision while he was in Asia, secretly admonished him, saying: "Come over to Macedonia and help us" (Acts 16:9). And in another place the same apostle said: "We are fellow workmen for God; you are God's tillage, God's building" (I Cor. 3:9).

Yet, on the other hand, we must beware that we do not attribute too much to ministers and the ministry; remembering here also the words of the Lord in the Gospel: "No one can come to me unless my Father draws him" (John 6:44), and the words of the apostle: "What then is Paul? What is Apollos? Servants through whom you believed, as the Lord assigned to each. I planted, Apollos watered, but only God gives the growth" (I Cor. 3:5 ff.).

GOD MOVES THE HEARTS OF MEN. Therefore, let us believe that God teaches us by his word, outwardly through his ministers, and inwardly moves the hearts of his elect to faith by the Holy Spirit; and that therefore we ought to render all glory unto God for this whole favor. But this matter has been dealt with in the first chapter of this Exposition.

WHO THE MINISTERS ARE AND OF WHAT SORT GOD HAS GIVEN TO THE WORLD. And even from the beginning of the world God has used the most excellent men in the whole world (even if many of them were simple in worldly wisdom or philosophy, but were outstanding in true theology), namely, the patriarchs, with whom he frequently spike by angels. For the patriarchs were the prophets or teachers of their age whom God for this reason wanted to live for several centuries, in order that they might be, as it were, fathers and lights of the world. They were followed by Moses and the prophets renowned throughout all the world.

CHRIST THE TEACHER. After these the heavenly Father even sent his only-begotten Son, the most perfect teacher of the world; in whom is hidden the wisdom of God, and which has come to us through the most holy, simple, and most perfect doctrine of all. For he chose disciples for himself whom he made apostles. These went out into the whole world, and everywhere gathered together churches by the preaching of the Gospel, and then throughout all the churches in the world they appointed pastors or teachers according to Christ's command; through their successors he has taught and governed the Church unto this day. Therefore, as God gave unto his ancient people the patriarchs, together with Moses and the prophets, so also to his people of the New Testament he sent his only-begotten Son, and, with him, the apostles and teachers of the Church.

MINISTERS OF THE NEW TESTAMENT. Furthermore, the ministers of the new people are called by various names. For they are called apostles, prophets, evangelists, bishops, elders, pastors, and teachers (I Cor. 12:28; Eph. 4:11).

THE APOSTLES. The apostles did not stay in any particular place, but throughout the world gathered together different churches. When they were once established, there ceased to be apostles, and pastors took their place, each in his church.

PROPHETS. In former times the prophets were seers, knowing the future; but they also interpreted the Scriptures. Such men are also found still today.

EVANGELISTS. The writers of the history of the Gospel were called Evangelists; but they also were heralds of the Gospel of Christ; as Paul also commended Timothy: "Do the work of an evangelist" (II Tim. 4:5).

BISHOPS. Bishops are the overseers and watchmen of the Church, who administer the food and needs of the life of the Church.

PRESBYTERS. The presbyters are the elders and, as it were, senators and fathers of the Church, governing it with wholesome counsel.

PASTORS The pastors both keep the Lord's sheepfold, and also provide for its needs.

TEACHERS. The teachers instruct and teach the true faith and godliness. Therefore, the ministers of the churches may now be called bishops, elders, pastors, and teachers.

PAPAL ORDERS. Then in subsequent times many more names of ministers in the Church were introduced into the Church of God. For some were appointed patriarchs, others archbishops, others suffragans; also, metropolitans, archdeacons, deacons, subdeacons, acolytes, exorcists, cantors, porters, and I know not what others, as cardinals, provosts, and priors; greater and lesser fathers, greater and lesser orders. But we are not troubled about all these about how they once were and are now. For us the apostolic doctrine concerning ministers is sufficient.

CONCERNING MONKS. Since we assuredly know that monks, and the orders or sects of monks, are instituted neither by Christ nor by the apostles, we teach that they are of no use to the Church of God, nay rather, are pernicious. For, although in former times they were tolerable (when they were hermits, earning their living with their own hands, and were not a burden to anyone, but like the laity were everywhere obedient to the pastors of the churches), yet now the whole world sees and knows what they are like. They formulate I know not what vows; but they lead a life quite contrary to their vows, so that the best of them deserves to be numbered among those of whom the apostle said: "We hear that some of you are living an irregular life, mere busybodies, not doing any work" etc. (II Thess. 3:11). Therefore, we neither have such in our churches, nor do we teach that they should be in the churches of Christ.

MINISTERS ARE TO BE CALLED AND ELECTED. Furthermore, no man ought to usurp the honor of the ecclesiastical ministry; that is, to seize it for himself by bribery or any deceits, or by his own free choice. But let the ministers of the Church be called and chosen by lawful and ecclesiastical election; that is to say, let them be carefully chosen by the Church or by those delegated from the Church for that purpose in a proper order without any uproar, dissension and rivalry. Not any one may be elected, but capable men distinguished by sufficient consecrated learning, pious eloquence, simple wisdom, lastly, by moderation and an honorable reputation, according to that apostolic rule which is compiled by the apostle in I Tim., ch. 3, and Titus, ch. 1.

ORDINATION. And those who are elected are to be ordained by the elders with public prayer and laying on of hands. Here we condemn all those who go off of their own accord, being nether chosen, sent, nor ordained (Jer., ch. 23). We condemn unfit ministers and those not furnished with the necessary gifts of a pastor.

In the meantime we acknowledge that the harmless simplicity of some pastors in the primitive Church sometimes profited the Church more than the many-sided, refined and fastidious, but a little too esoteric learning of others. For this reason we do not reject even today the honest, yet by no means ignorant, simplicity of some.

PRIESTHOOD OF ALL BELIEVERS. To be sure, Christ's apostles call all who believe in Christ "priests," but not on account of an office, but because, all the faithful having been made kings and priests, we are able to offer up a spiritual sacrifices to God through Christ (Ex. 19:6; I Peter 2:9; Rev. 1:6). Therefore, the priesthood and the ministry are very different from one another. For the priesthood, as we have just said, is common to all Christians; not so is the ministry. Nor have we abolished the ministry of the Church because we have repudiated the papal priesthood from the Church of Christ.

PRIESTS AND PRIESTHOOD. Surely in the new covenant of Christ there is no longer any such priesthood as was under the ancient people; which had an external anointing, holy garments, and very many ceremonies which were types of Christ, who abolished them all by this coming and fulfilling them. But he himself remains the only priest forever, and lest we derogate anything form him, we do not impart the name of priest to any minister. For the Lord himself did not appoint any priests in the Church of the New Testament who, having received authority from the suffragan, may daily offer up the sacrifice that is, the very flesh and blood of the Lord, for the living and the dead, but ministers who may teach and administer the sacraments.

THE NATURE OF THE MINISTERS OF THE NEW TESTAMENT. Paul explains simply and briefly what we are to think of the ministers of the New Testament or of the Christian Church, and what we are to attribute to them. "This is how one should regard us, as servants of Christ and stewards of the mysteries of God" II Cor. 4:1). Therefore, the apostle wants us to think of ministers as ministers. Now the apostle calls them rowers, who have their eyes fixed on the coxswain, and so men who do not live for themselves or according to their own will, but for others-- namely, their masters, upon whose command they altogether depend. For in all his duties every minister of the Church is commanded to carry out only what he has received in commandment from his Lord, and not to indulge his own free choice. And in this case it is expressly declared who is the Lord, namely, Christ; to whom the ministers are subject in all the affairs of the ministry.

MINISTERS AS STEWARDS OF THE MYSTERIES OF GOD. Moreover, to the end that he might expound the ministry more fully, the apostle adds that ministers of the Church are administrators and stewards of the mysteries of God. Now in may passages, especially in Eph., ch. 3, Paul called the mysteries of God the Gospel of Christ. And the sacraments of Christ are also called mysteries by the ancient writers. Therefore for this purpose are the ministers of the Church called--namely, to preach the Gospel of Christ to the faithful, and to administer the sacraments. We read, also, in another place in the Gospel, of "the faithful and wise steward," whom "his master will set over his household, to give them their portion of food at the proper time" (Luke 12:42). Again, elsewhere in the Gospel a man takes a journey in a foreign country and, leaving his house, gives his substance and authority over it to his servants, and to each his work.

THE POWER OF MINISTERS OF THE CHURCH. Now, therefore, it is fitting that we also say something about the power and duty of the ministers of the Church. Concerning this power some have argued industriously, and to it have subjected everything on earth, even the greatest things, and they have done so contrary to the commandment of the Lord who has prohibited dominion for this disciples and has highly commended humility (Luke 22:24 ff.; Matt. 18:3 f.; 20:25 ff.). There is, indeed, another power that is pure and absolute, which is called the power of right. According to this power all things in the whole world are subject to Christ, who is Lord of all, as he himself has testified when he said: "All authority in heaven and on earth has been given to me" (Matt. 28:18), and again, "I am the first and the last, and behold I am alive for evermore, and I have the keys of Hades and Death" (Rev. 1:18); also, "He has the key of David, which opens and no one shall shut, who shuts and no one opens" (Rev. 3:7).

THE LORD RESERVES TRUE POWER FOR HIMSELF. This power the Lord reserves to himself, and does not transfer it to any other, so that he might stand idly by as a spectator while his ministers work. For Isaiah says, "I will place on his shoulder the key of the house of David" (Isa. 22:22), and again, "The government will be upon his shoulders, but still keeps and uses his own power, governing all things.

THE POWER OF THE OFFICE AND OF THE MINISTER. Then there is another power of an office or of ministry limited by him who has full and absolute power. And this is more like a service than a dominion.

THE KEYS. For a lord gives up his power to the steward in his house, and for that cause gives him the keys, that he may admit into or exclude from the house those whom his lord will have admitted or excluded. In virtue of this power the minister, because of his office, does that which the Lord has commanded him to do; and the Lord confirms what he does, and wills that what his servant has done will be so regarded and acknowledges, as if he himself had done it. Undoubtedly, it is to this that these evangelical sentences refer: "I will give you the keys of the kingdom of heaven, and whatever you bind on earth shall be bound in heaven, and whatever you loose on earth shall be loosed in heaven" (Matt. 16:19). Again, "If you forgive the sins of any, they are forgiven; if you retain the sins of any, they are retained" (John 20:23). But if the minister does not carry out everything as the Lord has commanded him, but transgresses the bounds of faith, then the Lord certainly makes void what he has done. Wherefore the ecclesiastical power of the ministers of the Church is that function whereby they indeed govern the Church of God, but yet se do all things in the Church as the Lord has prescribed in his Word. When those things are done, the faithful esteem them as done by the Lord himself. But mention has already been made of the keys above.

THE POWER OF MINISTERS IS ONE AND THE SAME, AND EQUAL. Now the one and an equal power or function is given to all ministers in the Church. Certainly, in the beginning, the bishops or presbyters governed the Church in common; no man lifted up himself above another, none usurped greater power or authority over his fellow-bishops. For remembering the words of the Lord: "Let the leader among you become as one who serves" (Luke 22:26), they kept themselves in humility, and by mutual services they helped one another in the governing and preserving of the Church.

ORDER TO BE PRESERVED. Nevertheless, for the sake of preserving order some one of the ministers called the assembly together, proposed matters to be laid before it, gathered the opinions of the others, in short, to the best of man's ability took precaution lest any confusion should arise. Thus did St. Peter, as we read in The Acts of the Apostles, who nevertheless was not on that account preferred to the others, nor endowed with greater authority than the rest. Rightly then does Cyprian the Martyr say, in his De Simplicitate Clericorum: "The other apostles were assuredly what Peter was, endowed with a like fellowship of honor and power; but [his] primacy proceeds from unity in order that the Church may be shown to be one."

WHEN AND HOW ONE WAS PLACED BEFORE THE OTHERS. St. Jerome also in his commentary upon The Epistle of Paul to Titus, says something not unlike this: "Before attachment to persons in religion was begun at the instigation of the devil, the churches were governed by the common consultation of the elders; but after every one thought that those whom he had baptized were his own, and not Christ's, it was decreed that one of the elders should be chosen, and set over the rest, upon whom should fall the care of the whole Church, and all schismatic seeds should be removed." Yet St. Jerome does not recommend this decree as divine; for he immediately adds: "As the elders knew from the custom of the Church that they were subject to him who was set over them, so the bishops knew that they were subject to him who was set over them, so the bishops knew that they were above the elders, more from custom than from the truth of an arrangement by the Lord, and that they ought to rule the Church in common with them." Thus far St. Jerome. Hence no one can rightly forbid a return to the ancient constitution of the Church of God, and to have recourse to it before human custom.

THE DUTIES OF MINISTERS. The duties of ministers are various; yet for the most part they are restricted to two, in which all the rest are comprehended: to the teaching of the Gospel of Christ, and to the proper administration of the sacraments. For it is the duty of the ministers to gather together an assembly for worship in which to expound God's Word and to apply the whole doctrine to the care and use of the Church, so that what is taught may benefit the hearers and edify the faithful It falls to ministers, I say, to teach the ignorant, and to exhort; and to urge the idlers and lingerers to make progress in the way of the Lord. Moreover, they are to comfort and to strengthen the fainthearted, and to arm them against the manifold temptations of Satan; to rebuke offenders; to recall the erring into the way; to raise the fallen; to convince the gainsayers to drive the wolf away from the sheepfold of the Lord; to rebuke wickedness and wicked men wisely and severely; no to wink at nor to pass over great wickedness. And, besides, they are to administer the sacraments, and to commend the right use of them, and to prepare all men by wholesome doctrine to receive them; to preserve the faithful in a holy unity; and to check schisms; to catechize the unlearned, to commend the needs of the poor to the Church, to visit, instruct, and keep in the way of life the sick and those afflicted with various temptations. In addition, they are to attend to public prayers of supplications in times of need, together with common fasting, that is, a holy abstinence; and as diligently as possible to see to everything that pertains to the tranquility, peace and welfare of the churches.

But in order that the minister may perform all these things better and more easily, it is especially required of him that he fear God, be constant in prayer, attend to spiritual reading, and in all things and at all times be watchful, and by a purity of life to let his light to shine before all men.

DISCIPLINE. And since discipline is an absolute necessity in the Church and excommunication was once used in the time of the early fathers, and there were ecclesiastical judgments among the people of God, wherein this discipline was exercised by wise and godly men, it also falls to ministers to regulate this discipline for edification, according to the circumstances of the time, public state, and necessity. At all times and in all places the tule is to be observed that everything is to be done for edification, decently and honorably, without oppression and strife. For the apostle testifies that authority in the Church was given to him by the Lord for building up and not for destroying (II Cor. 10:8). And the Lord himself forbade the weeds to be plucked up in the Lord's field, because there would be danger lest the wheat also be plucked up with it (Matt. 13:29 f.).

EVEN EVIL MINISTERS ARE TO BE HEARD. Moreover, we strongly detest the error of the Donatists who esteem the doctrine and administration of the sacraments to be either effectual or not effectual, according to the good or evil life of the ministers. For we know that the voice of Christ is to be heard, though it be out of the mouths of evil ministers; because the Lord himself said: "Practice and observe whatever they tell you, but not what they do" (Matt. 23:3). We know that the sacraments are sanctified by the institution and the word of Christ, and that they are effectual to the godly, although they be administered by unworthy ministers. Concerning this matter, Augustine, the blessed servant of God, many times argued from the Scriptures against the Donatists.

SYNODS. Nevertheless, there ought to be proper discipline among ministers. In synods the doctrine and life of ministers is to be carefully examined. Offenders who can be cured are to be rebuked by the elders and restored to the right way, and if they are incurable, they are to be deposed, and like wolves driven away from he flock of the Lord by the true shepherds. For, if they be false teachers, they are not to be tolerated at all. Neither do we disapprove of ecumenical councils, if they are convened according to the example of the apostles, for the welfare of the Church and not for its destruction.

THE WORKER IS WORTHY OF HIS REWARD. All faithful ministers, as good workmen, are also worthy of their reward, and do not sin when they receive a stipend, and all things that be necessary for themselves and their family. For the apostle shows in I Cor., ch. 9, and in I Tim., ch. 5, and elsewhere that these things may rightly be given by the Church and received by ministers. The Anabaptists, who condemn and defame ministers who live from their ministry are also refuted by the apostolic teaching.

OF THE SACRAMENTS OF THE CHURCH OF CHRIST

THE SACRAMENTS [ARE] ADDED TO THE WORD AND WHAT THEY ARE. From the beginning, God added to the preaching of his Word in his Church sacraments or sacramental signs. For thus does all Holy Scripture clearly testify. Sacraments are mystical symbols, or holy rites, or sacred actions, instituted by God himself, consisting of his Word, of signs and of things signified, whereby in the Church he keeps in mind and from time to time recalls the great benefits he has shown to men; whereby also he seals his promises, and outwardly represents, and, as it were, offers unto our sight those things which inwardly he performs for us, and so strengthens and increases our faith through the working of God's Spirit in our hearts. Lastly, he thereby distinguishes us from all other people and religions, and consecrates and binds us wholly to himself, and signifies what he requires of us.

SOME ARE SACRAMENTS OF THE OLD, OTHERS OF THE NEW, TESTAMENTS. Some sacraments are of the old, others of the new, people. The sacraments of the ancient people were circumcision, and the Paschal Lamb, which was offered up; for that reason it is referred to the sacrifices which were practiced from the beginning of the world.

THE NUMBER OF SACRAMENTS OF THE NEW PEOPLE. The sacraments of the new people are Baptism and the Lord's Supper. There are some who count seven sacraments of the new people. Of these we acknowledge that repentance. the ordination of ministers (not indeed the papal but apostolic ordination), and matrimony are profitable ordinances of God, but not sacraments. Confirmation and extreme unction are human inventions which the Church can dispense with without any loss, and indeed, we do not have them in our churches. For they contain some things of which we can by no means approve. Above all we detest all the trafficking in which the Papists engage in dispensing the sacraments.

THE AUTHOR OF THE SACRAMENTS. The author of all sacraments is not any man, but God alone. Men cannot institute sacraments. For they pertain to the worship of God, and it is not for man to appoint and prescribe a worship of God, but to accept and preserve the one he has received from God. Besides, the symbols have God's promises annexed to them, which require faith. Now faith rests only upon the Word of God; and the Word of God is like papers or letters, and the sacraments are like seals which only God appends to the letters.

CHRIST STILL WORKS IN SACRAMENTS. And as God is the author of the sacraments, so he continually works in the Church in which they are rightly carried out; so that the faithful, when they receive them from the ministers, know that God works in his own ordinance, and therefore they receive them as from the hand of God; and the minister's faults (even if they be very great) cannot affect them, since they acknowledge the integrity of the sacraments to depend upon the institution of the Lord.

THE SUBSTANCE OR CHIEF THING IN THE SACRAMENTS. But the principal thing which God promises in all sacraments and to which all the godly in all ages direct their attention (some call it the substance and matter of sacraments) is Christ the Savior -- that only sacrifice, and that Lamb of God slain from the foundation of the world; that rock, also, from which all our fathers drank, by whom all the elect are circumcised without hands through the Holy Spirit, and are washed from all their sins, and are nourished with the very body and blood of Christ unto eternal life.

THE SIMILARITY AND DIFFERENCE IN THE SACRAMENTS OF OLD AND NEW PEOPLES. Now, in respect of that which is the principal thing and the matter itself in the sacraments, the sacraments of both peoples are equal. For Christ, the only Mediator and Savior of the faithful, is the chief thing and very substance of the sacraments in both; for the one God is the author of them both. They were given to both peoples as signs and seals of the grace and promises of God, which should call to mind and renew the memory of God's great benefits, and should distinguish the faithful from all the religions in the world; lastly, which should be received spiritually by faith, and should bind the receivers to the Church, and admonish them of their duty. In these and similar respects, I say, the sacraments of both peoples are not dissimilar, although in the outward signs they are different. And, indeed, with respect to the signs we make a great difference. For ours are more firm and lasting, inasmuch as they will never be changed to the end of the world. Moreover, ours testify that both the substance and the promise have been fulfilled or perfected in Christ; the former signified what was to be fulfilled. Ours are also more simple and less laborious, less sumptuous and involved with ceremonies. Moreover, they belong to a more numerous people. one that is dispersed throughout the whole earth. And since they are more excellent, and by the Holy Spirit kindle greater faith, a greater abundance of the Spirit also ensues.

OUR SACRAMENTS SUCCEED THE OLD WHICH ARE ABROGATED. But now since Christ the true Messiah is exhibited unto us, and the abundance of grace is poured forth upon the people of The New Testament, the sacraments of the old people are surely abrogated and have ceased; and in their stead the symbols of the New Testament are placed -- Baptism in the place of circumcision, the Lord's Supper in place of the Paschal Lamb and sacrifices.

IN WHAT THE SACRAMENTS CONSIST. And as formerly the sacraments consisted of the word, the sign, and the thing signified; so even now they are composed, as it were, of the same parts. For the Word of God makes them sacraments, which before they were not.

THE CONSECRATION OF THE SACRAMENTS. For they are consecrated by the Word, and shown to be sanctified by him who instituted them. To sanctify or consecrate anything to God is to dedicate it to holy uses; that is, to take it from the common and ordinary use, and to appoint it to a holy use. For the signs in the sacraments are drawn from common use, things external and visible. For in baptism the sign is the element of water, and that visible washing which is done by the minister; but the thing signified is regeneration and the cleansing from sins. Likewise, in the Lord's Supper, the outward sign is bread and wine, taken from things commonly used for meat and drink; but the thing signified is the body of Christ which was given, and his blood which was shed for us, or the communion of the body and blood of the Lord. Wherefore, the water, bread, and wine, according to their nature and apart from the divine institution and sacred use, are only that which they are called and we experience. But when the Word of God is added to them, together with invocation of the divine name, and the renewing of their first institution and sanctification, then these signs are consecrated, and shown to be sanctified by Christ. For Christ's first institution and consecration of the sacraments remains always effectual in the Church of God, so that these who do not celebrate the sacraments in any other way than the Lord himself instituted from the beginning still today enjoy that first and all-surpassing consecration. And hence in the celebration of the sacraments the very words of Christ are repeated.

SIGNS TAKE NAME OF THINGS SIGNIFIED. And as we learn out of the Word of God that these signs were instituted for another purpose than the usual use, therefore we teach that they now, in their holy use, take upon them the names of things signified, and are no longer called mere water, bread or wine, but also regeneration or the washing of water, and the body and blood of the Lord or symbols and sacraments of the Lord's body and blood. Not that the symbols are changed into the things signified, or cease to be what they are in their own nature. For otherwise they world not be sacraments. If they were only the thing signified, they would not be signs.

THE SACRAMENTAL UNION. Therefore the signs acquire the names of things because they are mystical signs of sacred things, and because the signs and the things signified are sacramentally joined together; joined together, I say, or united by a mystical signification, and by the purpose or will of him who instituted the sacraments. For the water, bread, and wine are not common, but holy signs. And he that instituted water in baptism did not institute it with the will and intention that the faithful should only be sprinkled by the water of baptism; and he who commanded the bread to be eaten and the wine to be drunk in the supper did not want the faithful to receive only bread and wine without any mystery as they eat bread in their homes; but that they should spiritually partake of the things signified, and by faith be truly cleansed from their sins, and partake of Christ.

THE SECTS. And, therefore, we do not at all approve of those who attribute the sanctification of the sacraments to I know not what properties and formula or to the power of words pronounced by one who is consecrated and who has the intention of consecrating, and to other accidental things which neither Christ or the apostles delivered to us by word or example. Neither do we approve of the doctrine of those who speak of the sacraments just as common signs, not sanctified and effectual. Nor do we approve of those who despise the visible aspect of the sacraments because of the invisible, and so believe the signs to be superfluous because they think they already enjoy the things themselves, as the Messalians are said to have held.

THE THING SIGNIFIED IS NEITHER INCLUDED IN OR BOUND TO THE SACRAMENTS. We do not approve of the doctrine of those who teach that grace and the things signified are so bound to and included in the signs that whoever participate outwardly in the signs, no matter what sort of persons they be, also inwardly participate in the grace and things signified.

However, as we do not estimate the value of the sacraments by the worthiness or unworthiness of the ministers, so we do not estimate it by the condition of those who receive them. For we know that the value of the sacraments depends upon faith and upon the truthfulness and pure goodness of God. For as the Word of God remains the true Word of God, in which, when it is preached, not only bare words are repeated, but at the same time the things signified or announced in words are offered by God, even if the ungodly and unbelievers hear and understand the words yet do not enjoy the things signified, because they do not receive them by true faith; so the sacraments, which by the Word consist of signs and the things signified, remain true and inviolate sacraments, signifying not only sacred things, but, by God offering, the things signified, even if unbelievers do not receive the things offered. This is not the fault of God who gives and offers them, but the fault of men who receive them without faith and illegitimately; but whose unbelief does not invalidate the faithfulness of God (Rom. 3:3 f.).

THE PURPOSE FOR WHICH SACRAMENTS WERE INSTITUTED. Since the purpose for which sacraments were instituted was also explained in passing when right at the beginning of our exposition it was shown what sacraments are, there is no need to be tedious by repeating what once has been said. Logically, therefore, we now speak severally of the sacraments of the new people.

OF HOLY BAPTISM

THE INSTITUTION OF BAPTISM. Baptism was instituted and consecrated by God. First John baptized, who dipped Christ in the water in Jordan. From him it came to the apostles, who also baptized with water. The Lord expressly commanded them to preach the Gospel and to baptize "in the name of the Father and of the Son and of the Holy Spirit" (Matt. 28:19). And in The Acts, Peter said to the Jews who inquired what they ought to do: "Be baptized every one of you in the name of Jesus Christ for the forgiveness of your sins; and you shall receive the gift of the Holy Spirit" (Acts 2:37 f.). Hence by some baptism is called a sign of initiation for God's people, since by it the elect of God are consecrated to God.

ONE BAPTISM. There is but one baptism in the Church of God; and it is sufficient to be once baptized or consecrated unto God. For baptism once received continues for all of life, and is a perpetual sealing of our adoption.

WHAT IT MEANS TO BE BAPTIZED. Now to be baptized in the name of Christ is to be enrolled, entered, and received into the covenant and family, and so into the inheritance of the sons of God; yes, and in this life to be called after the name of God; that is to say, to be called a son of God; to be cleansed also from the filthiness of sins, and to be granted the manifold grace of God, in order to lead a new and innocent life. Baptism, therefore, calls to mind and renews the great favor God has shown to the race of mortal men. For we are all born in the pollution of sin and are the children of wrath. But God, who is rich in mercy, freely cleanses us from our sins by the blood of his Son, and in him adopts us to be his sons, and by a holy covenant joins us to himself, and enriches us with various gifts, that we might live a new life. All these things are assured by baptism. For inwardly we are regenerated, purified, and renewed by God through the Holy Spirit and outwardly we receive the assurance of the greatest gifts in the water, by which also those great benefits are represented, and, as it were, set before our eyes to be beheld.

WE ARE BAPTIZED WITH WATER. And therefore we are baptized, that is, washed or sprinkled with visible water. For the water washes dirt away, and cools and refreshes hot and tired bodies. And the grace of God performs these things for souls, and does so invisibly or spiritually.

THE OBLIGATION OF BAPTISM. Moreover, God also separates us from all strange religions and peoples by the symbol of baptism, and consecrates us to himself as his property. We, therefore, confess our faith when we are baptized, and obligate ourselves to God for obedience, mortification of the flesh, and newness of life. Hence, we are enlisted in the holy military service of Christ that all our life long we should fight against the world, Satan, and our own flesh. Moreover, we are baptized into one body of the Church, that with all members of the Church we might beautifully concur in the one religion and in mutual services.

THE FORM OF BAPTISM. We believe that the most perfect form of baptism is that by which Christ was baptized, and by which the apostles baptized. Those things, therefore, which by man's device were added afterwards and used in the Church we do not consider necessary to the perfection of baptism. Of this kind is exorcism, the use of burning lights, oil, salt, spittle, and such other things as that baptism is to be celebrated twice every year with a multitude of ceremonies. For we believe that one baptism of the Church has been sanctified in God's first institution, and that it is consecrated by the Word and is also effectual today in virtue of God's first blessing.

THE MINISTER OF BAPTISM. We teach that baptism should not be administered in the Church by women or midwives. For Paul deprived women of ecclesiastical duties, and baptism has to do with these.

ANABAPTISTS. We condemn the Anabaptists, who deny that newborn infants of the faithful are to be baptized. For according to evangelical teaching, of such is the Kingdom of God, and they are in the covenant of God. Why, then, should the sign of God's covenant not be given to them? Whey should those who belong to God and are in his Church not be initiated by holy baptism? We condemn also the Anabaptists in the rest of their peculiar doctrines which they hold contrary to the Word of God. We therefore are not Anabaptists and have nothing in common with them.

OF THE HOLY SUPPER OF THE LORD

THE SUPPER OF THE LORD. The Supper of the Lord (which is called the Lord's Table, and the Eucharist, that is, a Thanksgiving), is, therefore, usually called a supper, because it was instituted by Christ at this last supper, and still represents it, and because in it the faithful are spiritually fed and given drink.

THE AUTHOR AND CONSECRATOR OF THE SUPPER. For the author of the Supper of the Lord is not an angel or any man, but the Son of God himself, our Lord Jesus Christ, who first consecrated it to his Church. And the same consecration or blessing still remains among all those who celebrate no other but that very Supper which the Lord instituted, and at which they repeat the words of the Lord's Supper, and in all things look to the one Christ by a true faith, from whose hands they receive, as it were, what they receive through the ministry of the ministers of the Church.

A MEMORIAL OF GOD'S BENEFITS. By this sacred rite the Lord wishes to keep in fresh remembrance that greatest benefit which he showed to mortal men, namely, that by having given his body and shed his blood he has pardoned all our sins, and redeemed us from eternal death and the power of the devil, and now feeds us with his flesh, and gives us his blood to drink, which, being received spiritually by true faith, nourish us to eternal life. And this so great a benefit is renewed as often as the Lord's Supper is celebrated. For the Lord said: "Do this in remembrance of me." This holy Supper also seals to us that the very body of Christ was truly given for us, and his blood shed for the remission of our sins, lest our faith should in any way waver.

THE SIGN AND THING SIGNIFIED. And this is visibly represented by this sacrament outwardly through the ministers, and, as it were, presented to out eyes to be seen, which is invisibly wrought by the Holy Spirit inwardly in the soul. Bread is outwardly offered by the minister, and the words of the Lord are heard: "Take, eat; this is my body"; and, "Take and divide among you. Drink of it, all of you; this is my blood." Therefore the faithful receive what is given by the ministers of the Lord, and they eat the bread of the Lord and drink of the Lord's cup. At the same time by the work of Christ through the Holy Spirit they also inwardly receive the flesh and blood of the Lord, and are thereby nourished unto life eternal. For the flesh and blood of Christ is the true food and drink unto life eternal; and Christ himself, since he was given for us and is our Savior, is the principal thing in the Supper, and we do not permit anything else to be substituted in his place.

But in order to understand better and more clearly how the flesh and blood of Christ are the food and drink of the faithful, and are received by the faithful unto eternal life, we would add these few things. There is more than one kind of eating. There is corporeal eating whereby food is taken into the mouth, is chewed with the teeth, and swallowed into the stomach. In times past the Capernaites thought that the flesh of the Lord should be eaten in this way, but they are refuted by him in John, ch. 6. For as the flesh of Christ cannot be eaten corporeally without infamy and savagery, so it is not food for the stomach. All men are forced to admit this. We therefore disapprove of that canon in the Pope's decrees, Ego Berengarius (De Consecrat., Dist. 2). For neither did godly antiquity believe, nor do we believe, that the body of Christ is to be eaten corporeally and essentially with a bodily mouth.

SPIRITUAL EATING OF THE LORD. There is also a spiritual eating of Christ's body; not such that we think that thereby the food itself is to be changed into spirit, but whereby the body and blood of the Lord, while remaining in their own essence and property, are spiritually communicated to us, certainly not in a corporeal but in a spiritual way, by the Holy Spirit, who applies and bestows upon us these things which have been prepared for us by the sacrifice of the Lord's body and blood for us, namely, the remission of sins, deliverance, and eternal life; so that Christ lives in us and we live in him, and he causes us to receive him by true faith to this end that he may become for us such spiritual food and drink, that is, our life.

CHRIST AS OUR FOOD SUSTAINS US IN LIFE. For even as bodily food and drink not only refresh and strengthen our bodies, but also keeps them alive, so the flesh of Christ delivered for us, and his blood shed for us, not only refresh and strengthen our souls, but also preserve them alive, not in so far as they are corporeally eaten and drunken, but in so far as they are communicated unto us spiritually by the Spirit of God, as the Lord said: "The bread which I shall give for the life of the world is my flesh (John 6:51), and "the flesh" (namely what is eaten bodily) "is of no avail; it is the spirit that gives life" (v. 63). And: "The words that I have spoken to you are spirit and life."

CHRIST RECEIVED BY FAITH. And as we must by eating receive food into our bodies in order that it may work in us, and prove its efficacy in us -- since it profits us nothing when it remains outside us -- so it is necessary that we receive Christ by faith, that he may become ours, and he may live in us and we in him. For he says: "I am the bread of life; he who comes to me shall not hunger, and he who believes in me shall never thirst" (John

6:35); and also, "He who eats me will live because of me...he abides in me, I in him" (vs. 57, 56).

SPIRITUAL FOOD. From all this it is clear that by spiritual food we do not mean some imaginary food I know not what but the very body of the Lord given to us, which nevertheless is received by the faithful not corporeally, but spiritually by faith. In this matter we follow the teaching of the Savior himself, Christ the Lord, according to John, ch. 6.

EATING NECESSARY FOR SALVATION. And this eating of the flesh and drinking of the blood of the Lord is so necessary for salvation that without it no man can be saved. But this spiritual eating and drinking also occurs apart from the Supper of the Lord, and as often and wherever a man believes in Christ. To which that sentence of St. Augustine's perhaps applies: "Why do you provide for your teeth and your stomach? Believe, and you have eaten."

SACRAMENTAL EATING OF THE LORD. Besides the higher spiritual eating there is also a sacramental eating of the body of the Lord by which not only spiritually and internally the believer truly participates in the true body and blood of the Lord, but also, by coming to the Table of the Lord, outwardly receives the visible sacrament of the body and blood of the Lord. To be sure, when the believer believed, he first received the life-giving food, and still enjoys it. But therefore, when he now received the sacrament, he does not received nothing. For he progresses in continuing to communicate in the body and blood of the Lord, and so his faith is kindle and grows more and more, and is refreshed by spiritual food. For while we live, faith is continually increased. And he who outwardly receives the sacrament by true faith, not only receives the sign, but also, as we said, enjoys the thing itself. Moreover, he obeys the Lord's institution and commandment, and with a joyful mind gives thanks for his redemption and that of all mankind, and makes a faithful memorial to the Lord's death, and gives a witness before the Church, of whose body he is a member. Assurance is also given to those who receive the sacrament that the body of the Lord was given and his blood shed, not only for men in general, but particularly for every faithful communicant, to whom it is food and drink unto eternal life.

UNBELIEVERS TAKE THE SACRAMENT TO THEIR JUDGMENT. But he who comes to this sacred Table of the Lord without faith, communicates only in the sacrament and does not receive the substance of the sacrament whence comes life and salvation; and such men unworthily eat of the Lord's Table. Whoever eats the bread or drinks the cup of the Lord in an unworthy manner will be guilty of the body and blood of the Lord, and eats and drinks judgment upon himself (I Cor. 11:26-29). For when they do not approach with true faith, they dishonor the death of Christ, and therefore eat and drink condemnation to themselves.

THE PRESENCE OF CHRIST IN THE SUPPER. We do not, therefore, so join the body of the Lord and his blood with the bread and wine as to say that the bread itself is the body of Christ except in a sacramental way; or that the body of Christ is hidden corporeally under the bread, so that it ought to be worshipped under the form of bread; or yet that whoever receives the sign, receives also the thing itself. The body of Christ is in heaven at the right hand of the Father; and therefore our hearts are to be lifted up on high, and not to be fixed on the bread, neither is the Lord to be worshipped in the bread. Yet the Lord is not absent from his Church when she celebrates the Supper. The sun, which is absent from us in the heavens, is notwithstanding effectually present among us. How much more is the Sun of Righteousness, Christ, although in his body he is absent from us in heaven, present with us, not corporeally, but spiritually, by his vivfying operation, and as he himself explained at his Last Supper that he world be present with us (John, chs. 14; 15; and 16). Whence it follows that we do not have the Supper without Christ, and yet at the same time have an unbloody and mystical Supper, as it was universally called by antiquity.

OTHER PURPOSES OF THE LORD'S SUPPERS. Moreover, we are admonished in the celebration of the Supper of the Lord to be mindful of whose body we have become members, and that, therefore, we may be of one mind with all the brethren, live a holy life, and not pollute ourselves with wickedness and strange religions; but, perservering in the true faith to the end of our life, strive to excel in holiness of life.

PREPARATION FOR THE SUPPER. It is therefore fitting that when we would come to the Supper, we first examine ourselves according to the commandment of the apostle, especially as to the kind of faith we have, whether we believe that Christ has come to save sinners and to call them to repentance, and whether each man believes that he is in the number of those who have been delivered by Christ and saved; and whether he is determined to change his wicked life, to lead a holy life, and with the Lord's help to persevere in the true religion and in harmony with the brethren, and to give due thanks to God for his deliverance.

THE OBSERVANCE OF THE SUPPER WITH BOTH BREAD AND WINE. We think that rite, manner, or form of the Supper to be the most simple and excellent which comes nearest to the first institution of the Lord and to the apostles' doctrine. It consists in proclaiming the Word of God, in godly prayers, in the action of the Lord himself, and its repetition, in the eating of the Lord's body and drinking of this blood; in a fitting remembrance of the

Lord's death, and a faithful thanksgiving; and in a holy fellowship in the union of the body of the Church.

We therefore disapprove of those who have taken from the faithful one species of the sacrament, namely, the Lord's cup. For these seriously offend against the institution of the Lord who says: "Drink ye all of this"; which he did not so expressly say of the bread.

We are not now discussing we what kind of mass once existed among the fathers, whether it is to be tolerated or not. But this we say freely that the mass which is now used throughout the Roman Church has been abolished in our churches for many and very good reasons which, for brevity's sake, we do not now enumerate in detail. We certainly could not approve of making a wholesome action into a vain spectacle and a means of giving merit, and of celebrating it for a price. Nor could we approve of saying that in it the priest is said to effect the very body of the Lord, and really to offer it for the remission of the sins of the living and the dead, and in addition, for the honor, veneration and remembrance of the saints in heaven, etc.

OF RELIGIOUS AND ECCLESIASTICAL MEETINGS

WHAT OUGHT TO BE DONE IN MEETINGS FOR WORSHIP. Although it is permitted all men to read the Holy Scriptures privately at home, and by instruction to edify one another in the true religion, yet in order that the Word of God may be properly preached to the people, and prayers and supplication publicly made, also that the sacraments may be rightly administered, and that collections may be made for the poor and to pay the cost of all the Church's expenses, and in order to maintain social intercourse, it is most necessary that religious or Church gatherings be held. For it is certain that in the apostolic and primitive Church, there were such assemblies frequented by all the godly.

MEETINGS FOR WORSHIP NOT TO BE NEGLECTED. As many as spun such meetings and stay away from them, despise true religion, and are to be urged by the pastors and godly magistrates to abstain from stubbornly absenting themselves from sacred assemblies.

MEETINGS ARE PUBLIC. But Church meetings are not to be secret and hidden, but public and well attended, unless persecution by the enemies of Christ and the Church does not permit them to be public. For we know how under the tyranny of the Roman emperors the meetings of the primitive Church were held in secret places.

DECENT MEETING PLACES. Moreover, the places where the faithful meet are to be decent, and in all respects fit for God's

Church. Therefore, spacious buildings or temples are to be chosen, but they are to be purged of everything that is not fitting for a church. And everything is to be arranged for decorum, necessity, and godly decency, lest anything be lacking that is required for worship and the necessary works of the Church.

MODESTY AND HUMILITY TO BE OBSERVED IN MEETINGS. And as we believe that God does not dwell in temples made with hands, so we know that on account of God's Word and sacred use places dedicated to God and his worship are not profane, but holy, and that those who are present in them are to conduct themselves reverently and modestly, seeing that they are in a sacred place, in the presence of God and his holy angels.

THE TRUE ORNAMENTATION OF SANCTUARIES. Therefore, all luxurious attire, all pride, and everything unbecoming to Christian humility, discipline and modesty, are to be banished from the sanctuaries and places of prayer of Christians. For the true ornamentation of churches does not consist in ivory, gold, and precious stones, but in the frugality, piety, and virtues of those who are in the Church. Let all things be done decently and in order in the church, and finally, let all things be done for edification.

WORSHIP IN THE COMMON LANGUAGE. Therefore, let all strange tongues keep silence in gatherings for worship, and let all things be set forth in a common language which is understood by the people gathered in that place.

OF THE PRAYERS OF THE CHURCH, OF SINGING, AND OF CANONICAL HOURS

COMMON LANGUAGE. It is true that a man is permitted to pray privately in any language that he understands, but public prayers in meetings for worship are to be made in the common language known to all.

PRAYER. Let all the prayers of the faithful be poured forth to God alone, through the mediation of Christ only, out of faith and love. The priesthood of Christ the Lord and true religion forbid the invocation of saints in heaven or to use them as intercessors. Prayer is to be made for magistracy, for kings, and all that are placed in authority, for ministers of the Church, and for all needs of churches. In calamities, especially of the Church, unceasing prayer is to be made both privately and publicly.

FREE PRAYER. Moreover, prayer is to be made voluntarily, without constraint or for any reward. Nor is it proper for prayer to be superstitiously restricted to one place, as if it were not permitted to pray anywhere except in a sanctuary. Neither is it necessary for public prayers to be the same in all churches with respect to form and time. Each Church is to exercise its own freedom. Socrates, in his history, says, "In all regions of the world you will not find two churches which wholly agree in prayer" (Hist. ecclesiast. V.22, 57). The authors of this difference, I think, were those who were in charge of the Churches at particular times. Yet if they agree, it is to be highly commended and imitated by others.

THE METHOD TO BE EMPLOYED IN PUBLIC PRAYERS. As in everything, so also in public prayers there is to be a standard lest they be excessively long and irksome. The greater part of meetings for worship is therefore to be given to evangelical teaching, and care is to be taken lest the congregation is wearied by too lengthy prayers and when they are to hear the preaching of the Gospel they either leave the meeting or, having been exhausted, want to do away with it altogether. To such people the sermon seems to be overlong, which otherwise is brief enough. And therefore it is appropriate for preachers to keep to a standard.

SINGING. Likewise moderation is to be exercised where singing is used in a meeting for worship. That song which they call the Gregorian Chant has many foolish things in it; hence it is rightly rejected by many of our churches. If there are churches which have a true and proper sermon but no singing, they ought not to be condemned. For all churches do not have the advantage of singing. And it is well known form testimonies of antiquity that the custom of singing is very old in the Eastern Churches whereas it was late when it was at length accepted in the West.

CANONICAL HOURS. Antiquity knew nothing of canonical hours, that is, prayers arranged for certain hours of the day, and sung or recited by the Papists, as can be proved from their breviaries and by many arguments. But they also have not a few absurdities, of which I say nothing else; accordingly they are rightly omitted by churches which substitute in their place things that are beneficial for the whole Church of God.

OF HOLY DAYS, FASTS AND THE CHOICE OF FOODS

THE TIME NECESSARY FOR WORSHIP. Although religion is not bound to time, yet it cannot be cultivated and exercised without a proper distribution and arrangement of time. Every Church, therefore, chooses for itself a certain time for public prayers, and for the preaching of the Gospel, and for the celebration of the sacraments; and no one is permitted to overthrow this appointment of the Church at his own pleasure. For unless some due time and leisure is given for the outward exercise of religion, without doubt men would be drawn away from it by their own affairs.

THE LORD'S DAY. Hence we see that in the ancient churches there were not only certain set hours in the week appointed for meetings, but that also the Lord's Day itself, ever since the apostles' time, was set aside for them and for a holy rest, a practice now rightly preserved by our Churches for the sake of worship and love.

SUPERSTITION. In this connection we do not yield to the Jewish observance and to superstitions. For we do not believe that one day is any holier than another, or think that rest in itself is acceptable to God. Moreover, we celebrate the Lord's Day and not the Sabbath as a free observance.

THE FESTIVALS OF CHRIST AND THE SAINTS. Moreover, if in Christian liberty the churches religiously celebrate the memory of the Lord's nativity, circumcision, passion, resurrection, and of his ascension into heaven, and the sending of the Holy Spirit upon his disciples, we approve of it highly. but we do not approve of feasts instituted for men and for saints. Holy days have to do with the first Table of the Law and belong to God alone. Finally, holy days which have been instituted for the saints and which we have abolished, have much that is absurd and useless, and are not to be tolerated. In the meantime, we confess that the remembrance of saints, at a suitable time and place, is to be profitably commended to the people in sermons, and the holy examples of the saints set forth to be imitated by all.

FASTING. Now, the more seriously the Church of Christ condemns surfeiting, drunkenness, and all kinds of lust and intemperance, so much the more strongly does it commend to us Christian fasting. For fasting is nothing else than the abstinence and moderation of the godly, and a discipline, care and chastisement of our flesh undertaken as a necessity for the time being, whereby we are humbled before God, and we deprive the flesh of its fuel so that it may the more willingly and easily obey the Spirit. Therefore, those who pay no attention to such things do not fast, but imagine that they fast if they stuff their stomachs once day, and at a certain or prescribed time abstain from certain foods, thinking that by having done this work they please God and do something good. Fasting is an aid to the prayers of the saints and for all virtues. But as is seen in the books of the prophets, the fast of the Jews who fasted from food but not from wickedness did not please God.

PUBLIC AND PRIVATE FASTING. Now there is a public and a private fasting. In olden times they celebrated public fasts in calamitous limes and in the affliction of the Church. They abstained altogether from food till the evening, and spent all that time in holy prayers, the worship Of God, and repentance These differed little from mourning, and there is frequent mention of them in the Prophets and especially by Joel in Ch. 2.

Such a fast should be kept at this day, when the Church is in distress. private fasts are undertaken by each one of us, as he feels himself withdrawn from the Spirit. For in this manner he withdraws the flesh from its fuel.

CHARACTERISTICS OF FASTING. All fasts ought to proceed from a free and willing spirit, and from genuine humility, and not feigned to gain the applause or favor of men, much less that a man should wish to merit righteousness by them. But let every one fast to this end, that he may deprive the flesh of its fuel in order that he may the more zealously serve God.

LENT. The fast of Lent is attested by antiquity but not at all in the writings of the apostles. Therefore it ought not, and cannot, be imposed on the faithful. It is certain that formerly there were various forms and customs of fasting. hence, Irenaeus, a most ancient writer, says: "Some think that a fast should be observed one day only, others two days, but others more, and some forty days. This diversity in keeping this fast did not first begin in our times, but long before us by those, as I suppose, who did not simply keep to what had been delivered to them from the beginning, but afterwards fell into another custom either through negligence or ignorance" (Fragm. 3, ed. Stieren, I. 824 f.). Moreover, Socrates, the historian, says: "Because no ancient text is found concerning this matter, I think the apostles left this to every man's own judgment, that every one might do what is good without fear or constraint" (Hist. ecclesiast. V.22, 40).

CHOICE OF FOOD. Now concerning the choice of foods, we think that in fasting all things should be denied to the flesh whereby the flesh is made more insolent, and by which it is greatly pleased, and by which it is inflamed with desire whether by fish or meat or spices or delicacies and excellent wines. Moreover, we know that all the creatures of God were made for the use and service of men. All things which God made are good, and without distinction are to be used in the fear of God and with proper moderation (Gen. 2:15 f.). For the apostle says: "To the pure all things are pure" (Titus 1:15), and also: "Eat whatever is sold in the meat market without raising any question on the ground of conscience" (I Cor. 10:25). The same apostle calls the doctrine of those who teach to abstain form meats "the doctrine of demons"; for "God created foods to be received with thanksgiving by those who believe and know this truth that everything created by God is good, and nothing is to be rejected if it is received with thanksgiving" (I Tim. 4:1 ff.) The same apostle, in the epistle to the Colossians, reproves those who want to acquire a reputation for holiness by excessive abstinence (Col. 2:18 ff.).

SECTS. Therefore we entirely disapprove of the Tatians and the Encratites, and all the disciples of Eustathius, against whom the Gangrain Synod was called.

OF CATECHIZING AND OF COMFORTING AND VISITING THE SICK

YOUTH TO BE INSTRUCTED IN GODLINESS. The Lord enjoined his ancient people to exercise the greatest care that young people, even from infancy, be properly instructed. Moreover, he expressly commanded in his law that they should teach them, and that the mysteries of the sacra-ments should be explained. Now since it is well known from the writings of the Evangelists and apostles that God has no less concern for the youth of his new people, when he openly testifies and says: "Let the children come to me; for to such belongs the kingdom of heaven" (Mark 10:14), the pastors of the churches act most wisely when they early and carefully caetchize the youth, laying the first grounds of faith, and faithfully teaching the rudiments of our religion by expounding the Ten Commandments, the Apostles' Creed, the Lord's Prayer, and the doctrine of the sacraments, with other such principles and chief heads of our religion. Here let the Church show her faith and diligence in bringing the children to be catechized, desirous and glad to have her children well instructed.

THE VISITATION OF THE SICK. Since men are never exposed to more grievous temptations than when they are harassed by infirmities, are sick and are weakened by diseases of both soul and body, surely it is never more fitting for pastors of churches to watch more carefully for the welfare of their flocks than in such diseases and infirmities. Therefore let them visit the sick soon, and let them be called in good time by the sick, if the circumstance itself would have required it. Let them comfort and confirm them in the true faith, and then arm them against the dangerous suggestions of Satan. They should also hold prayer for the sick in the home and, if need be, prayers should also be made for the sick in the public meeting; and they should see that they happily depart this life. We said above that we do not approve of the popish visitation of the sick with extreme unction because it is absurd and is not approved by canonical Scriptures.

OF THE BURIAL OF THE FAITHFUL, AND OF THE CARE TO BE SHOWN FOR THE DEAD; OF PURGATORY, AND THE APPEARING OF SPIRITS

THE BURIAL OF BODIES. As the bodies of the faithful are the temples of the Holy Spirit which we truly believe will rise again at the Last Day, Scriptures command that they be honorably and without superstition committed to the earth, and also that honorable mention be made of those saints who have fallen asleep in the Lord, and that all duties of familial piety be shown to those left behind, their widows and orphans. We do not teach that any other care be taken for the dead. Therefore, we greatly disapprove of the Cynics, who neglected the bodies of the dead or most carelessly and disdainfully cast them into the earth, never saying a good word about the deceased, or caring a bit about those whom they left behind them.

THE CARE FOR THE DEAD. On the other hand, we do not approve of those who are overly and absurdly attentive to the deceased; who, like the heathen, bewail their dead (although we do not blame that moderate mourning which the apostle permits in I Thess. 4:13, judging it to be inhuman not to grieve at all); and who sacrifice for the dead, and mumble certain prayers for pay, in order by such ceremonies to deliver their loved ones from the torments in which they are immersed by death, and then think they are able to liberate them by such incantations.

THE STATE OF THE SOUL DEPARTED FROM THE BODY. For we believe that the faithful, after bodily death, go directly to Christ, and, therefore, do not need the eulogies and prayers of the living for the dead and their services. Likewise we believe that unbelievers are immediately cast into hell from which no exit is opened for the wicked by any services of the living.

PURGATORY. But what some teach concerning the fire of purgatory is opposed to the Christian faith, namely, "I believe in the forgiveness of sins, and the life everlasting," and to the perfect purgation through Christ, and to these words of Christ our Lord: "Truly, truly, I say to you, he who hears my word and believes him who sent me, has eternal life; he shall not come into judgment, but has passed from death to life" (John 5:24). Again: "He who has bathed does not need to wash, except for his feet, but he is clean all over, and you are clean" (John 13:10).

APPARITION OF SPIRITS. Now what is related of the spirits or souls of the dead sometimes appearing to those who are alive, and begging certain duties of them whereby they may be set free, we count those apparitions among the laughingstocks, crafts, and deceptions of the devil, who, as he can transform himself into an angel of light, so he strives either to overthrow the true faith or to call it into doubt. In the Old Testament the Lord forbade the seeking of the truth from the dead, and any sort of commerce with spirits Deut. 18:11). Indeed, as evangelical truth declares, the glutton, being in torment, is denied a return to his brethren, as the divine oracle declared in the words: "They have Moses and the prophets; let them hear them. If they hear not Moses and the prophets, neither will they be convinced if some one should rise from the dead" (Luke 16:29 ff.).

OF RITES, CEREMONIES AND THINGS INDIFFERENT

CEREMONIES AND RITES. Unto the ancient people were given at one time certain ceremonies, as a kind of instruction for those who were kept under the law, as under a schoolmaster or tutor. But when Christ, the Deliverer, came and the law was abolished, we who believe are no more under the law (Rom. 6:14), and the ceremonies have disap-peared; hence the apostles did not want to retain or to restore them in Christ's Church to such a degree that they openly testified that they did not wish to impose any burden upon the Church. Therefore, we would seem to be bringing in and restoring Judaism if we were to increase ceremonies and rites in Christ's Church according to the custom in the ancient Church. Hence, we by no means approve of the opinion of those who think that the Church of Christ must be held in check by many different rites, as if by some kind of training. For if the apostles did not want to impose upon Christian people ceremonies or rites which were appointed by God, who, I pray, in his right mind would obtrude upon them the inventions devised by man? The more the mass of rites is increased in the Church, the more is detracted not only from Christian liberty, but also from Christ, and from faith in him, as long as the people seek those things in ceremonies which they should seek in the only Son of God, Jesus Christ, through faith. Wherefore a few moderate and simple rites, that are not contrary to the Word of God, are sufficient for the godly.

DIVERSITY OF RITES. If different rites are found in churches, no one should think that for this reason the churches disagree.

Socrates says: "It would be impossible to put together in writing all the rites of churches throughout cities and countries. No religion observes the same rites, even though it embraces the same doctrine concerning them. For those who are of the same faith disagree among themselves about rites" (Hist. ecclesiast. V.22, 30, 62). This much says Socrates. And we, today, having in our churches different rites in the celebration of the Lord's Supper and in some other things, nevertheless do not disagree in doctrine and faith; nor is the unity and fellowship of our churches thereby rent asunder. For the churches have always used their liberty in such rites, as being things indifferent. We also do the same thing today.

THINGS INDIFFERENT. But at the same time we admonish me to be on guard lest they reckon among things indifferent what are in fact not indifferent, as some are wont to regard the mass and the use of images in places of worship as things indifferent. "Indifferent," wrote Jerome to Augustine, "is that which is neither good nor bad, so that, whether you do it or not, you are neither just nor unjust." Therefore, when things indifferent are wrested to the confession of faith, they cease to be free; as Paul shows that it is lawful for a man to eat flesh if someone does not remind him that it was offered to idols; for then it is unlawful, because he who eats it seems to approve idolatry by eating it (I Cor. 8:9 ff.; 10:25 ff.).

OF THE POSSESSIONS OF THE CHURCH

THE POSSESSIONS OF THE CHURCH AND THEIR PROPER USE. The Church of Christ possesses riches through the munificence of princes and the liberality of the faithful who have given their means to the Church. For the Church has need of such resources and from ancient time has had resources for the maintenance of things necessary for the Church. Now the true use of the Church's wealth was, and is now, to maintain teaching in schools and in religious meetings, along with all the worship, rites, and buildings of the Church; finally, to maintain teachers, scholars, and ministers, with other necessary things, and especially for the succor and relief of the poor.

MANAGEMENT. Moreover, God-fearing and wise men, noted for the management of domestic affairs, should be chosen to administer properly the Church's possessions.

THE MISUSE OF THE CHURCH'S POSSESSIONS. But if through misfortune or through the audacity, ignorance or avarice of some persons the Church's wealth is abused, it is to be restored to a sacred use by godly and wise men. For neither is an abuse, which is the greatest sacrilege, to be winked at. Therefore, we teach that schools and institutions which have been corrupted in doctrine, worship and morals must be reformed, and that the relief of the poor must be arranged dutifully, wisely, and in good faith.

OF CELIBACY, MARRIAGE AND THE MANAGEMENT OF DOMESTIC AFFAIRS

SINGLE PEOPLE. Those who have the gift of celibacy from heaven, so that from the heart or with their whole soul are pure and continent and are not aflame with passion, let them serve the Lord in that calling, as long as they feel endued with that divine gift; and let them not lift up themselves above others, but let them serve the Lord continuously in simplicity and humility (I Cor. 7:7 ff.). For such are more apt to attend to divine things than those who are distracted with the private affairs of a family. But if, again, the gift be taken away, and they feel a continual burning, let them call to mind the words of the apostle: "It is better to marry than to be aflame" (I Cor. 7:9).

MARRIAGE. For marriage (which is the medicine of incontinency, and continency itself) was instituted by the Lord God himself, who blessed it most bountifully, and willed man and woman to cleave one to the other inseparable, and to live together in complete love and concord (Matt. 19:4 ff.). Whereupon we know that the apostle said: "Let marriage be held in honor among all, and let the marriage bed be undefiled" (Heb. 13:4). And again: "If a girl marries, she does not sin" (I Cor. 7:28).

THE SECTS. We therefore condemn polygamy, and those who condemn second marriages.

HOW MARRIAGES ARE TO BE CONTRACTED. We teach that marriages are to be lawfully contracted in the fear of the Lord, and not against the laws which forbid certain degrees of consanguinity, lest the marriages should be incestuous. Let marriages be made with consent of the parents, or of those who take the place of parents, and above all for that purpose for which the Lord instituted marriages. Moreover, let them be kept holy with the utmost faithfulness, piety, love and purity of those joined together. Therefore let them guard against quarrels, dissensions, lust and adultery.

MATRIMONIAL FORUM. Let lawful courts be established in the Church, and holy judges who may care for marriages, and may repress all unchastity and shamefulness, and before whom matrimonial disputes may be settled.

THE REARING OF CHILDREN. Children are to be brought up by the parents in the fear of the Lord; and parents are to provide for their children, remembering the saying of the apostle: "If anyone does not provide for his relatives, he has disowned the faith and is worse than an unbeliever" (I Tim. 5:8). But especially they should teach their children honest trades or professions by which they may support themselves. They should ;keep them from idleness and in all these things instill in them true faith in God, lest through a lack of confidence or too much security or filthy greed they become dissolute and achieve no success.

And it is most certain that those works which are done by parents in true faith by way of domestic duties and the management of their households are in God's sight holy and truly good works. They are no less pleasing to God than prayers, fasting and almsgiving. For thus the apostle has taught in his epistles, especially in those to Timothy and Titus. And with the same apostle we account the doctrine of those who forbid marriage or openly castigate or indirectly discredit it, as if it were not holy and pure, among the doctrine of demons.

We also detest an impure single life, the secret and open lusts and fornications of hypocrites pretending to be continent when they are the most incontinent of all. All these God will judge. We do not disapprove of riches or rich men, if they be godly and use their riches well. But we reject the sect of the Apostolicals (The Apostolicals were followers of a religious fanatic, Gherardo Segarelli, of Parma, who in the thirteenth century wanted to restore the poverty of the apostolic life.)

OF THE MAGISTRACY

THE MAGISTRACY IS FROM GOD. Magistracy of every kind is instituted by God himself for the peace and tranquillity of the human race, and thus it should have the chief place in the world. If the magistrate is opposed to the Church, he can hinder and disturb it very much; but if he is a friend and even a member of the Church, he is a most useful and excellent member of it, who is able to benefit it greatly, and to assist it best of all.

THE DUTY OF THE MAGISTRATE. The chief duty of the magistrate is to secured and preserve peace and public tranquillity. Doubtless he will never do this more successfully than when he is truly God-fearing and religious; that is to say, when, according to the example of the most holy kings and princes of the people of the Lord, he promotes the preaching of the truth and sincere faith, roots out lies and all superstition, together with all impiety and idolatry, and defends the Church of God. We certainly teach that the care of religion belongs especially to the holy magistrate.

Let him, therefore, hold the Word of God in his hands, and take care lest anything contrary to it is taught. Likewise let him govern the people entrusted to him by God with good laws made according to the Word of God, and let him keep them in discipline, duty and obedience. Let him exercise judgment by judging uprightly. Let him not respect any man's person or accept bribes. Let him protect widows, orphans and the afflicted. Let him punish and even banish criminals, impostors and barbarians. For he does not bear the sword in vain (Rom. 13:4).

Therefore, let him draw this sword of God against all malefactors, seditious persons, thieves, murderers, oppressors, blasphemers, perjured persons, and all those whom God has commanded him to punish and even to execute. Let him suppress stubborn heretics (who are truly heretics), who do not cease to blaspheme the majesty of God and to trouble, and even to destroy the Church of God.

WAR. And if it is necessary to preserve the safety of the people by war, let him wage war in the name of God; provided he has first sought peace by all means possible, and cannot save his people in any other way except by war. And when the magistrate does these things in faith, he serves God by those very works which are truly good, and receives a blessing from the Lord.

We condemn the Anabaptists, who when they deny that a Christian may hold the office of a magistrate, deny also that a man may be justly put to death by the magistrate, or that the magistrate may wage war, or that oaths are to be rendered to a magistrate, and such like things.

THE DUTY OF SUBJECTS. For as God wants to effect the safety of his people by the magistrate, whom he has given to the world to be, as it were, a father, so all subjects are commanded to acknowledge this favor of God in the magistrate. Therefore let them honor and reverence the magistrate as the minister of God; let them love him, favor him, and pray for him as their father; and let them obey all his just and fair commands. Finally, let them pay all customs and taxes, and all other such dues faithfully and willingly. And if the public safety of the country and justice require it, and the magistrate of necessity wages war, let them even lay down their life and pour out their blood for the public safety and that of the magistrate. And let them do this in the name of God willingly, bravely and cheerfully. For he who opposes the magistrate provokes the severe wrath of God against himself.

SECTS AND SEDITIONS. We, therefore, condemn all who are contemptuous of the magistrate - rebels, enemies of the state, seditious villains, finally, all who openly or craftily refuse to perform whatever duties they owe.

We beseech God, our most merciful Father in heaven, that he will bless the rulers of the people, and us, and his whole people, through Jesus Christ, our only Lord and Savior; to whom be praise and glory and thanksgiving, for all ages. Amen.

www.ingramcontent.com/pod-product-compliance
Lightning Source LLC
Chambersburg PA
CBHW051549010526
44118CB00022B/2640